The Book of *Job*

LIVES OF GREAT RELIGIOUS BOOKS

FORTHCOMING:

The Book of *Job*

A BIOGRAPHY

Mark Larrimore

PRINCETON UNIVERSITY PRESS

Princeton and Oxford

Copyright © 2013 by Princeton University Press

Published by Princeton University Press, 41 William Street,

Princeton, New Jersey 08540

In the United Kingdom: Princeton University Press, 6 Oxford Street,

Woodstock, Oxfordshire OX20 1TW

press.princeton.edu

Figure 10 shows scripture taken from the NEW AMERICAN
STANDARD BIBLE®, © Copyright 1960, 1962, 1963, 1968, 1971,
1972, 1973, 1975, 1977, 1995 by The Lockman Foundation. Used by
permission. www.Lockman.org

Library of Congress Cataloging-in-Publication Data
    Larrimore, Mark J. (Mark Joseph), 1966–
    The Book of Job : a biography / Mark Larrimore.
        pages   cm. — (Lives of great religious books)
    Includes bibliographical references and index.
    ISBN 978-0-691-14759-8 (hardcover : alk. paper)   1. Bible. Job—
Criticism, interpretation, etc.   I. Title.
    BS1415.52.L37 2013
    223'.106—dc23

                                                    2013007556

British Library Cataloging-in-Publication Data is available

This book has been composed in Garamond Premier Pro

Printed on acid-free paper. ∞

Printed in the United States of America

10 9 8 7 6 5 4 3 2 1

CONTENTS

FIGURES

The Book of *Job*

Introduction

The book of Job tells of a wealthy and virtuous man in an unfamiliar land in the East. His virtue is so great that God points him out to *hassatan*— literally the *satan*, "the adversary," a sort of prose-cuting attorney in the divine court, who, whether by temperament or profession, is skeptical regard-ing the possibility of genuine human piety. (This is not the Satan with a capital S of later scriptural works and related lore and legend, although the two are soon identified.) This adversary argues that Job's piety is only the result of divine favor. If God stripped him of his good fortune, Job would curse God to his face. God lets the accuser destroy Job's wealth and kill his children. When even this pro-duces no more than the pious refrain "the Lord has given and the Lord takes away" from his servant, God lets the satan afflict Job with a terrible disease.

Job's wife counsels him to "curse God and die," but he remains steadfast in his piety.

In what some see as a final trial, three friends of Job arrive—Eliphaz, Bildad, and Zophar. They hardly recognize him. They sit with him in silence for seven days. Eventually Job speaks—and at this point the text moves from prose to poetry. In fact, Job curses. Yet he curses not God but the day of his birth. This provokes or permits his friends to speak, so one after another they try to make sense of his affliction. They all subscribe to versions of a retributionist view that sees suffering as divine punishment for iniquity, and they counsel Job to confess to sins, even ones he may not have known he committed, or ones committed by his children. Job, certain he has not sinned so grievously as to deserve such punishment, responds to each friend, with confusion that grows into anger. Afflicted by his friends' failure to recognize his innocence, Job increasingly addresses his words to God, whom he would like to call before a court. Many elements of a court case are imagined, including a *go'el*, a kind of advocate or champion who might vindicate Job, even if Job has by that time died. Job's speeches, each in a different mood, culminate in an assertion of innocence and a demand for a fair hearing, but also in the discovery that his case is not exceptional: the innocent suffer all the time in God's world.

After three cycles of speeches by the friends and responses by Job (the third friend speaks only twice), a hymn is delivered that sings of the inaccessibility of wisdom, and a new character speaks up, a young man named Elihu. Elihu provides his own account of what is happening: God sometimes tests the righteous, but always offers some resources to help them. Job does not respond, or doesn't get a chance. God now speaks from a whirlwind. In two powerful speeches reciting the marvels and the terrors of nature, God draws attention to the structures of creation and to some of its frightening denizens, including the giant beasts Behemoth and Leviathan. Job's questions about his own case and about the injustice of human life in general are not addressed. After each speech Job makes a kind of concession, the second ending with a tangle of words that is difficult to translate. The most well-known rendering:

I had heard of you by the hearing of the ear,
    but now my eye sees you;
therefore I despise myself,
    and repent in dust and ashes.[1]

The narrative returns to prose as God addresses the three friends (not Elihu) and condemns them for not speaking rightly as Job has. They are commanded to offer sacrifices, which must be conducted by Job. Job's life is restored. New children are born and Job receives twice the wealth of before, living out his days in happiness.

The book of Job is often understood as the Bible's answer to the problem of evil. Many find in it the Bible's deepest reflections on the meaning of suffering. Others see it as monotheism's admission of moral bankruptcy, posing a question so difficult that even God cannot answer it. G. K. Chesterton thought even God was tempted to atheism in the book of Job, and C. G. Jung thought God suffered such a moral defeat at Job's hands that he had to assume human form and sacrifice himself in order to recoup. It is remarkable that a single book should impress such different kinds of people. Indeed, readers are so uniform in their praise of its sublime power that one recent commentator has been led to wonder if it isn't a work of ideology, religiously mystifying injustices of a more mundane kind: it just kicks problems of human injustice upstairs, making it easier for us to ignore them.[2]

Job is concerned that he not be ignored:

Oh, that my words were written down!
O that they were inscribed in a book!
O that with an iron pen and with lead
they were engraved on a rock forever!
(19:23–24)

Job wants his story to be a book, and every interpreter has tried to be the bookbinder. Yet the book
of Job resists being corralled into a single interpretation. Orthodox interpreters have an especially hard
time: Job says things they find difficult to accept.
The pious asseverations of Job's friends, condemned
by God, are the passages in the book of Job that best
square with other texts accepted as scriptural. But
the book of Job trips up modernizing readings, too,
not least with its apparently bullying God.

There is a sense in which any interpretation of
a text renders it a book. Any reading, no matter
how sympathetic or disruptive, brings a more explicit order to the text. But Job's words at 19:23–
24 are a particularly helpful way of thinking about
the drama of interpreters' attempts to befriend the
book of Job. Job's friends get it wrong, after all, and
are restored to grace only by Job's sacrifice for them.
Job's wish to write his own book prevents us from
thinking we have made final sense of his story, even
as the book of Job suggests Job's own words may be
inadequate to the task, too.

This biography of the book of Job follows the
book as it was read and used, fought over, defended,
and reimagined. Our method will be to explore
various interpreters' attempts to make sense of this
Gordian knot of a text. The sequence of chapters is
loosely chronological, but the main concern of each

is to explore the career of a different set of interpretive strategies. While some may seem arcane, each can show us enduring possibilities within the book of Job. Each way of reading brings to bear assumptions not only about the book of Job but about the work of interpretation itself. Some of these assumptions will strike us as arbitrary, outmoded, or even capricious. Yet we will learn more from the book of Job if we explore all these different approaches. We need all the help we can find.

The book of Job arguably has more puzzles than any other book of the Bible. It starts and ends in prose, but the speeches of Job, his friends, and God are in poetry. It has many *hapax legomena*—words appearing nowhere but here—as well as passages of such great obscurity that interpreters have sometimes felt obliged to change letters to make any sense of them. (Some of the most influential passages, 13:15, 19:27, and 42:6, are among the most opaque.) Nevertheless, this challenging text has remained unchanged for a very long time. The Masoretes, the Jewish scholars who in the five centuries starting in the seventh century CE set about producing an authorized text of the Hebrew scriptures, found little meaningful variation among the manuscripts at their disposal. The Targum of Job, found in the library of Qumran (Dead Sea Scrolls), largely aligns with the Masoretic text (see figure 1).

Figure 1. The Aramaic Targum (paraphrase) of Job was among the texts found at Qumran known as the Dead Sea Scrolls. As for many of the texts found here, it largely coincides with the Masoretic text, which became canonical. This fragment corresponds to Job 41:25–42:6. Photograph by Bruce and Kenneth Zuckerman, West Semitic Research. Courtesy Israel Antiquities Authority. Collection of the Israel Antiquities Authority.

The only significant variant is found in the Greek translation of the Bible known as the Septuagint. This rendition of the book of Job has streamlined some of the speeches between Job and his friends and softened some of the language asserting God's agency in Job's trials. Essentially unchanged, however, are the puzzles and profundities that we will trace, challenges that arise from the larger shape and structure of the work as much as from its details. There are two interesting additions to the text,

however. Job's wife, who has only one line in the canonical text,[3] here is allowed to speak:

> How long will you persist and say, "Look, I will
> hang on a little longer, while I wait for the hope
> of my deliverance." For look, your legacy has
> vanished from the earth—sons and daughters,
> my womb's birth pangs and labors, for whom
> I wearied myself with hardships in vain. And
> you? You sit in the refuse of worms as you spend
> the night in the open air. As for me, I am one
> that wanders about and a hired servant—from
> place to place and house to house, waiting for
> when the sun will set, so I can rest from the dis-
> tresses and griefs that have now beset me. Now
> say some word to the Lord and die!" (2:9–9e)[4]

Also added is a genealogical appendix, showing Job
to be "the fifth from Abraam" (42:17a–d).[5] This
lineage draws explicitly on "the Syriac book," the
translation of the Bible known as the Peshitta, an
attribution which confirms that even at that time,
more widely used versions did not connect Job to
the story of the people of Israel.

Although the oldest versions are in agreement,
the troubled text on which they agree nevertheless appears to be corrupted in at least two ways.
First, it seems not to be of a piece but to have been
composed of distinct parts that do not fit together

entirely happily. The speeches of Elihu and the "Hymn to Wisdom" look most like insertions in this respect, but incongruities between the frame narrative and the poetic dialogue might suggest composite authorship on the largest scale. We'll discuss the implications of these possibilities, as well as of the different understandings of textual meaning and integrity that attend them, in chapter 5. Second, pieces of the text seem to have gone missing, and what survives seems in places to have been mixed up. Job's responses to the friends' speeches sometimes sound out of sync with them. In other cases, he takes up arguments it might seem he should be rejecting. A widely shared interpretation we'll see in chapter 5 recommends rearranging sections of Chapter 27. A recent Christian commentary moves the "Hymn to Wisdom" into the speeches of Elihu.[6]

Awareness of the composite character of a text inevitably changes the way we understand its meaning and its effective history. This awareness need not undermine the value of interpretations from eras unaware of the text's history, however. Readings that hinge on Elihu's speeches (like most of the important medieval Jewish commentaries[7]) or on the "Hymn to Wisdom" (like that in the recent *Africa Bible Commentary*[8]) may seem exercises in futility, doomed to irrelevance. But the relation between

Job's parts is more complicated than mere incompatibility. Its incongruities, however they came to be, are now a part of the text. The widespread view that the prose frame and the poetic dialogues are irreconcilable, thus forcing any reader implicitly or explicitly to choose one over the other, is itself an interpretation and, like any interpretation, a simplification.

Similar concerns attend what are now seen as mistranslations—*hassatan* as "Satan," or *goel* as "redeemer" among the most significant. And yet there are more reasons than mere anachronism to set aside this knowledge in reading the history of pre-modern interpretation. It is the book of Job as it was found that shaped our traditions. Early readers were fully aware of the difficulties around its interpretation. This is one reason none of them thought it possible to read the book of Job on its own. However uneasily it fits, the book of Job comes to us as part of the greater whole of scripture—Jewish or Christian— and has long been understood in that context. Pruning it so it can stand on its own is another interpretive intervention. We are increasingly coming to understand that the multiplicity of voices may be constitutive of the power of the book of Job. Indeed, so effectively do its voices complicate each other that it may be understood as a polyphonic whole, perhaps even the work of a single ingenious author.[9]

If the text is pretty certain, for all its rough edges, its origins are anything but. Premodern commentators wondered who wrote it: Job himself, perhaps, or Moses? Robert Lowth, the father of modern literary studies of the Bible, was sure it was the work of Moses, and also thought its language proved that it was the oldest text of the Bible.[10] But archaizing language is a genre of its own, and a Hebrew author familiar with Aramaic could explain at least some of the linguistic variety. The text may show familiarity with some texts of the Hebrew Bible, notably some of the Psalms and the creation story in Genesis, which Job seems to invert when he curses the day of his birth in Chapter 3. References to historically datable Sabean raids (1:15) and the gold of Ophir (22:24) provide a *terminus ante quem*, the latest the book—or at least the passages in which they appear—could have been written. Already in the Talmud it was suggested that the book of Job was written during the period of the Babylonian captivity, although hypotheses were offered linking it to the concerns of many other periods as well. Here as elsewhere the historical and interpretive tasks cannot be so easily distinguished.

Even finding a home for the book of Job in the Bible is harder than it might seem. There are two scriptural references to Job that have for centuries been taken as proof that he belonged, but neither seems to refer to the protagonist of the *book* of Job. The prophet Ezekiel refers to three men whose piety was so great that their lands were protected by it:

Mortal, when a land sins against me by acting faithlessly, and I stretch out my hand against it, and break its staff of bread and send famine upon it, and cut off from it human beings and animals, even if Noah, Daniel, and Job, these three, were in it, they would save only their own lives by their righteousness, says the Lord GOD. (Ezekiel 14:13–14)

This hardly sounds like the story of the Job we read of in the book of Job, even the pious Job of the prose tale, for his righteousness was the cause of his children's destruction! (Ezekiel's Daniel, too, is not the biblical seer but seems better associated with a Canaanite king named Dan'el known from tablets in late second millennium BCE Ugarit.) More fundamentally, the book of Job seems, of all the books of the Bible, to be least interested in and invested in the dependence of individuals and communities on each other's virtue. There may have been an ancient Job, but the story told in the book of Job seems to have been crafted later, perhaps even as a riposte to the ancient story.

The brief New Testament Epistle of James pro-vides a second but equally problematic biblical at-testation of Job:

> As an example of suffering and patience, be-loved, take the prophets who spoke in the name of the Lord. Indeed we call blessed those who showed endurance. You have heard of the pa-tience of Job, and you have seen the purpose of the Lord, how the Lord is compassionate and merciful. (James 5:10–11)

Patience is not mentioned in the book of Job, however—nor is prophecy. James may be referring explicitly to an oral tradition: "you have *heard* . . ."[11] The book of Job has always been accompanied by what has been called the "legend of Job," in which superlative patience is indeed Job's defining trait.[12] (We will see fruits of this tradition in chapters 1 and 3.) The legend may have come first, the book of Job (or at least its poetic diatribes) added by way of angry satiric subversion. The story of the patient Job was strong enough to lead the early fifth cen-tury commentator Theodore of Mopsuestia to ar-gue against the canonicity of the book of Job. He thought the now scriptural account to be a slander on the name of a historical hero.

The still idiomatic "patience of Job" is a good example of a Job interpretation we should handle with care. It's not enough to notice that the Job of the poetic dialogues seems to us far more "impatient" than "patient." Many contemporary interpreters who see the book of Job as composed of incompatible prose and poetic sections even distinguish them in these terms, pitting "Job the patient" against "Job the impatient." As we will see in chapter 5, the "impatience of Job" is well on its way to becoming proverbial, too. Still, what is translated as "patience" in the Epistle of James can perhaps more accurately be rendered "persistence" or "steadfastness" or "endurance."

It may be that James wasn't referring to the Job of "The Lord gave, and the Lord has taken away" (1:21) as opposed to the Job who grieves and curses and rails, but to both. Reading the reference to Job in context, James may not have been recommending a passive resignation but its opposite, what has been called a "militant patience."[13] Instead of rejecting the "patient Job" of the frame story, we might do better to rethink our conception of "patience." Abraham teaches us as no philosophical argument could what faith is; Job may do the same for patience.

Maybe the attitude of persistent Job, insisting on justice, is not impatience but true patience. The narrator's assurance that Job "didn't sin with his lips" (2:10) and God's claim (twice) that Job had

"spoken of me what is right" (42:6, 7) led premodern readers to see the book of Job as demonstrating
just how much a patient person *could* say without
sinning. Those responsible for the appropriation of
Job's speeches for the Christian burial liturgy understood that the book of Job defines the param-
eters of patience. There are registers of religious
expression—such as lament and protest—that saccharine modern understandings of religion can no
longer imagine.

Another way of anchoring Job in the Bible is
to fit him into its historical narrative, but without
something like the Septuagint's genealogical ad-
dendum this proves difficult as well. Job is from the
Land of Uz: could he have lived in the land of the
firstborn son of Abraham's brother Nahor, whose
name was Uz (Genesis 22:21)? And there is a Jobab
mentioned in a lineage of kings of Edom descended
of Esau (Genesis 36:33–34), though if this Jobab
did anything of note, it is not mentioned. He comes
and goes within a verse. What difference could so
passing a reference in Genesis make for Job?

In fact, the question of whether Job was a Jew
or a Gentile was an important one to both Jewish
and Christian interpreters—for different but not
unrelated reasons.[14] Being a lineal descendant of
Esau would be no prize, but at least it would make
Job a distant relation of the family of Israel. More

than one loose end is tied up by the teaching that Job's second wife was Jacob's daughter Dinah, another victim of biblical trauma, who disappeared from the biblical text after her rape and her brothers' revenge (Genesis 34). If Job was an outsider to the covenanted community, at least his descendants were not. A non-Israelite Job implies the possibility of access to God outside of the covenant. As we'll see in chapter 4, his place outside the covenantal community will help Job become a key figure in modern thought as well. Like a modern, he seems to have a relationship with God on his own and through conduct alone, unmediated by covenants, sacred law, or communal rituals.

Research on ancient analogs and sources is also of limited help in fixing Job's time, form, or authorship. There are texts, ranging from ancient Egypt to Babylon and the Hittites, which seem to overlap with one or another aspect of Job's story—a divine test, a pious man and his friends, a discussion of providence—but nothing similar enough to suggest a clear source or direct parallel.[15] The book of Job is evidently in conversation with what scholars have since the late nineteenth century called the "wisdom" tradition: a cosmopolitan intellectual tradition focused on the meaning of individual experience in this world, outside the context of specific religious narratives or traditions. But it is difficult to say more. At this remove it is impossible defini- tively to distinguish participation in a genre from a parody or attack on it.[16]

Many premodern commentators thought the riddle of Job could be answered if one could dis- cern its genre: epic, perhaps, or tragedy? Its happy resolution might even classify it as a comedy. Several genres do seem to be at play in the book of Job, but as a whole it is *sui generis*. However its components came about or were brought together, the resulting text has asserted itself as a whole, complete with ten- sions, for two and a half millennia. Its recalcitrance has become part of its mystique and, on some read- ings, of its message. Whether one thinks that divine providence is inscrutable or that Job's suffering is be- yond words, the text's resistance to final interpreta- tion and classification strengthens its force.

The role of the Job interpreter is thus not an easy one. Short of repeating the whole text verbatim, as one of Søren Kierkegaard's awestruck protagonists proposed,[17] what can she do? The text is involved, or conflicted, or rich, or barbed, or ironic, or inspired, or corrupt enough that no reader is truly comfort- able with everything in it. Whether we connect this with a notion of authorial intention or not, it is part of the enduring power of the work. The questions raised by the book of Job—providence and evil, the meaning of innocent suffering, the nature of God and humanity's place in creation, among the more obvious—are ones that resist closure.

In the narrative that follows I will highlight the assumptions various readers bring with them in working out their interpretations. This is not to accuse them of having hidden agendas. There are certainly better and worse readings of a text. Each makes use, in better or worse faith, of what she finds and interprets. The terms used—"figurative," "philosophical," "fragment"—are our terms, charged with our language and concerns. But this is only a problem if we ignore it. Trying to understand a text in relation to previous knowledge is part of any serious engagement with it. We are inclined to deny this basic condition of interpretation for a variety of reasons: the Reformation idea that the biblical text speaks unaided; the Enlightenment idea that we can set aside our prejudices; the Romantic idea that we can empathetically feel our way into a text; the Fundamentalist idea that meaning is literal and univocal; and the New Critical idea that each work of genius is its own world and must be allowed to be semantically autonomous.

It is particularly tempting to reject interpretations that appeal to preexisting belief since a central part of the drama of the book of Job is God's condemnation of Job's received wisdom-spouting friends. But Job himself offers no new way to speak.

One thing it might seem we can say is that an interpretation mustn't be allowed to displace the text itself. It seems unacceptable to change or omit passages one finds troublesome, as Stephen Mitchell does with his translation—but the Hellenistic Jews who generated the translation of the Septuagint did the same, and Hebraists remind us that in some passages of the book of Job the reader/translator has no choice but to intervene. Some of the pivotal moments in the book of Job are so obscure as to force even translators to interpret boldly.

A biography of the book of Job must not confine itself to readers, translators, commentators, and interpreters. The history of the reception of the book of Job is the history of its *use*. People turn to this text because it's part of a tradition, next up in a lectionary cycle or ritual manual. But they also turn to it in grief and confusion, in rage and existential crisis. The book of Job was more often heard than read; indeed, Job's was one of the most familiar biblical voices. Only rarely were such readings not structured by prayers, and interwoven with other texts. These were not understood as interruptions but as devices for disclosing the true meaning of the text—a meaning that went beyond the words on the page. No reader of the book of Job thinks it is possible to discuss theodicy (the problem of evil) dispassionately. The book is used in consolation, in self-help literature, in articulating confusion, and more. Its uses in liturgy, and in expressions and enactments of the oral traditions with which it shares its protagonist, must be part of our picture. Some of the book of Job's most interesting questions arise when it is performed.

While they are arranged in a roughly chronological order, the chapters of this book introduce ways of reading the book of Job that continue in one form or another into the present. There are distinct Jewish and Christian ways of reading scripture, and of reading Job in particular, but it seems more valuable here to suggest the ways in which the book of Job drove interpreters in many different contexts and traditions to some of the same kinds of inspiration, despair, and invention. It helps us situate ourselves more honestly to admit this, to admit Jewish, Platonist, Christian, Aristotelian as well as modern and postmodern presuppositions as our companions.

Chapter 1, "Job in the Ancient Interpreters," looks at efforts to read Job into the Bible by reading the Bible into Job. As we have seen, Job, Uz, and the rest are obscure, their relevance to the history of revelation uncertain. This chapter explores ways in which interpreters and commentators have made sense of the book of Job through etymologies, analogies, and contrasts—and engagement with the rival Jobs of legend and oral tradition. Chapter 2, "Job in Disputation," traces medieval interpretations of the book of Job as a philosophical discourse. The encounter of Job and his friends has been seen as representative of a wide array of disputing philosophical and theological views, and also of the conventions and limits of philosophical dispute itself—especially among friends. Chapter 3, "Job Enacted," follows the career of Job outside the text, probing his significance for the Christian burial ritual of the dead and his role in religious and non-liturgical performances. These premodern approaches to the book of Job are still vital to understanding the life of the book of Job.

Chapter 4, "Job in Theodicy," maps Job's iconic role in the emergence of modern western conceptions of religion grounded in the problem of theodicy—indeed in its insolubility—and the related thematics of the religious sublime. Chapter 5, "Job in Exile," explores the ways historical critical understandings have unsettled interpretations of Job, and the resonance a book now understood as fragmented has with considerations of the meaning of suffering and questions of justice and meaning after the Shoah, and more generally in a supposedly secular age. The Conclusion looks to the contemporary vitality of Joban interpretation in the modes discussed in past chapters, but also in some of the new contexts of global Christianity and western secularity.

The covers of most books about the book of Job depict Job or his God. More fitting for a biography of the book would be an image showing the different reactions of Job's comforters, who want to be friends to Job but ultimately fail. In a striking illumination from a ninth-century CE Byzantine Bible, for instance,[18] one friend weeps. Another tears his clothes in public sympathy. The third seems to cover his mouth in horror. The expression on his face may reflect the friends' initial inability to recognize Job in so woeful a state, or its overcoming. But he's probably also covering his nose at Job's stench. (In the modern age, most of us are innocent of the smell of physical decay and the visceral effect it can exert.) Job's debacle doesn't produce simple responses. And the book of Job warns us that what starts as companionable grief can become scapegoating betrayal.

We would do well to assume that all interpreters of Job come to the story as Job's friends do. We are not Job, and we do not know the mind of God or what goes on in his court. We come to this unbearable story with prejudgments and try to make sense of it with limited imaginations, the story cutting closer to home than we are comfortable acknowledging. The book of Job should teach us to expect failures of friendship, especially from ourselves. Part of the legacy of the book of Job has always been the way it empowers strong opinions. It is as much the friend of the accused heretic as of the accuser. It empowers sufferers, both patient and angry, critics of orthodoxy, and defenders of mysteries. We must be careful not to condemn them in the same way as those "miserable comforters" who think they can understand Job without wondering why they themselves are spared.

Many interpreters, among them Gregory the Great, the pope whose commentary made the book of Job one of the most important works of the Christian Middle Ages, considered themselves called to the study of Job by a life of physical pain: "perchance it was this that Divine Providence designed, that I, a stricken one, should set forth Job stricken, and that by these scourges I should the more perfectly enter into the feelings of one that was scourged."[19] Elie Wiesel, who saw a Job on every street of post–World War II Europe, can observe: "There were those who claimed that Job did exist but that his sufferings are sheer literary inventions. Then there were those who declared that while Job never existed, he undeniably did suffer."[20] Such readers know the realities of agony and abandonment, and how they can distort consciousness. I can claim no such interpretive privilege. From where I sit—not an ash heap but a college classroom—I see the book of Job appealing powerfully to those who know or suspect or fear that all is not right with the world, sufferers of many kinds. They turn to Job and his book for reassurance, but also for confirmation of the truth of their questions.

Some readers are put off by Job, but most want to take his side. Some readers are put off by Job's God. But almost all readers are put off by Job's friends, who seem the prototype of the adage, "with friends like these, who needs enemies?" And yet there is no place for *us* in the text except as friends, perhaps late arrivals like Elihu—though great has been the temptation to do better than Job's God. Part of the biography of the book of Job is the story of Job's friends over the centuries, readers who think they know and understand Job's sufferings, his character, and the meaning of his story. Some of these friends, at least, are mistaken. God reproves them for not speaking rightly. Friends, like interpretations, often disappoint, but it seems we cannot live without them. Job's friendships are the first part of his life to be restored after his calamity.

Introduction

Job in the Ancient Interpreters

CHAPTER 1

As modern readers informed by Enlightenment presuppositions and decades of historical critical scholarship, we think we know what the book of Job is and how to approach it. Like any other book, we assume it must be a fixed text with a beginning, middle, and end. We take for granted that it was written at a particular time by a particular person. We might (or might not) also ask for what purpose it was written. Knowing this is enough for us to know what the book is about, and to judge later interpretations and adaptations. We praise as legitimate those that illuminate things we too see in the text. We are skeptical of those that make claims that seem only weakly borne out by the text in question. And we dismiss, perhaps with disdain, those interpretations that interpret it in terms of things outside of it, especially if, as it seems to us, they at the same time ignore the plain meaning of the text.

All of these considerations impede our ability to assess early biblical interpreters. It looks to us as if they aren't reading the same text at all. So consistently do they miss what we think is the plain meaning that we suspect they're not even trying to read it faithfully. Indeed, they may seem to us willfully to ignore and obscure the meaning. In the case of the book of Job, the traditional "patient Job" reading seems to us to be painted over the actual story of Job, which is, at the very least, much more complicated.

The extent of early readers' ignoring or obscuring is much exaggerated, however. The result may appear obfuscatory, but they were trying to do something quite different from this. To appreciate what they were up to, we need to pluralize our sense of ways of reading—and of books. In this chapter we'll develop these new senses by looking at the book of Job as one of multiple renditions of a story, and as one of multiple texts in scripture. We'll explore the former through the *Testament of Job*, the most substantial residue of the popular and largely oral tradition sometimes known as the legend of Job. For the latter we'll look at the Talmud's midrashim on Job, and at Gregory the Great's moral and allegorical reading of Job. Each of these is doing something fundamentally different, and we need to dwell on those differences. But as a group they exemplify a distinctive way of approaching texts unfamiliar to us today which may yet have something to teach us. To help us shed the expectation that the book of Job is a clearly defined and self-interpreting piece of text, we start with a quick survey of the forms and settings in which it has been encountered over the centuries.

Books of Job

Whatever your image of the book of Job, it is probably a poor guide to understanding its history. We live in the only period in its history when it is widely available in translations without commentary and marketed on its own as a freestanding book. The materiality of independent binding might lead us to suppose the book of Job was always understood to be at least implicitly self-sufficient, but the story is quite different. The forms in which people encountered it emphasized that it was part of the library of scripture (*biblia* comes from the Greek word for books, plural) and, until very recently, was thought impossible to read unassisted.[1]

The Bible was never read in a linear way, one book following another, but the organization of its books remained significant and a subject of much discussion. In the Hebrew Bible, the Tanakh, the book of Job forms part of the third section, Ketu-bim (Writings); it often—but not always—came after Psalms and Proverbs and before the five Megil-lot or "little scrolls," the Song of Songs, Ruth, Lam-entations, Ecclesiastes, and Esther. It offers God's longest speech in scripture, and, in the chronology of the Tanakh, his last. If one read the Tanakh as if it were a biography of God, one might conclude that after the encounter with Job "God subsides," and that divine silence begins within, not after, the time of the Bible.[2]

The Christian Old Testament shares most books with the Tanakh but not their order. In the Tanakh the Ketubim is the last of three divisions, coming after Torah and Prophets. In Christian Bibles the Writings come between the Pentateuch and the Prophets. Read a Christian Old Testament from start to finish and you will not find God subsiding with Job. Through his prophets he has a lot more to say, all of it interpreted by Christian readers as setting the stage for the Christ. Many interpreters thought Job was a kind of prophet, too:

For I know that my Redeemer [go'el] lives,
    and that at the last he will stand upon the
    earth;
and after my skin has been thus destroyed,
    then in my flesh I shall see God,

whom I shall see on my side,
and my eyes shall behold, and not another.
(19:25-27a)

Job was also a "type" of Christ. "Job dolens inter-
pretatur, typum Christi ferebat," Jerome wrote:
Job's very name means sorrowing or suffering, and
he was a prefiguration of Christ.[3] As we will see
with Gregory the Great's *Morals in Job*, the man
from Uz's every word and gesture were understood
to anticipate the life and message of Christ.

While the Bible was regarded as the book par
excellence, the library of scripture wasn't a text like
others. For one thing, it didn't look like other texts.
The care taken in the writing, reading, and preser-
vation of Torah scrolls is well known. Elaborately
bound and beautifully scripted Christian codices
presented the Bible monumentally as well—and
not just because it was a great deal of text to present
between two covers.

Many manuscript Bibles were illustrated. The
book of Job offered artists many novel opportunities for visualization. The events of the destruction
of Job's life and livelihood were dramatic spectacles,
but the figurative language of the speeches that
make up the bulk of the text offered opportunities
of its own. The book of Job is distinguished among
biblical texts by the richness of the natural imagery

employed in its speeches, many of which were also understood allegorically. Byzantine illuminated Bibles show long-standing traditions and subtraditions in the representation of these figures and figurations.[4] These visual representations were important to the experience of the text even for those who could read. Much of the drama of Job concerns the limits of language and the power of representations that go beyond them.

For most of its history, encountering the biblical text on its own was as good as impossible. Scripture differed from merely human literary productions through a depth of meaning which demanded elaborate apparatuses of theological commentary. The clarifications of inspired and authorized interpreters were indispensable and the production of texts reflected this. Manuscripts and early printed editions of the Bible were often encased in so many layers of commentary that the words of the biblical text themselves seem mere islands in a sea of smaller, handwritten commentary. The twelfth century saw the emergence of a standardized synthesis of the commentaries that had been welling up around the margins and even between the lines of Christian Bibles, the *Glossa Ordinaria*. Approaching the text without reference to (or at least awareness of) the authoritative commentaries of church fathers and others was literally impossible. Commentary wasn't

Figure 2. The wealth of figurative language in the speeches in the book of Job provided opportunities for great artistic virtuosity. In this ninth-century Byzantine Bible known as *Vaticanus Graecus* we see Leviathan, the great sea monster, alongside the Septuagint text of 41:17–20. Image Vat.gr.749. - p.238r. Reproduced by permission of Biblioteca Apostolica Vaticana, with all rights reserved. © 2013 Biblioteca Apostolica Vaticana.

Job in the Ancient Interpreters   31

trying to bar access to the text, but to facilitate it (see figure 3).

How would a Christian reader in the Middle Ages have encountered Job? Jerome's pronouncement that Job means suffering and that he was a type of Christ was the entry point:

> Typically, approaching the beginning of Job, one is first greeted by a double prologue contributed by Jerome, one part bearing on the Septuagint and the other on the Hebrew text. This is followed by an *expositio* of the second part of the prologue and a double *praefatio* by Nicholas de Lyra, to which is appended an anonymous *additio*. Thereupon comes a somewhat lengthy "Prothemata in Job" based on Gregory's *Moralia*. Only now have we finally arrived at the first verse of the book of Job.[5]

Even then, it was slow going. Commentary illuminating the significance of the words "There was a man in the land of Uz by the name of Job" (1:1) took up several pages, as every word was parsed and reparsed. Our discussion of Gregory's *Morals in Job* will give a taste of the kind of significations offered.

Most people didn't have access to the Bible, and wouldn't have been able to read it if they had. The Bible was accessible to many more in visual form, and even in Bibles, images were more than mere

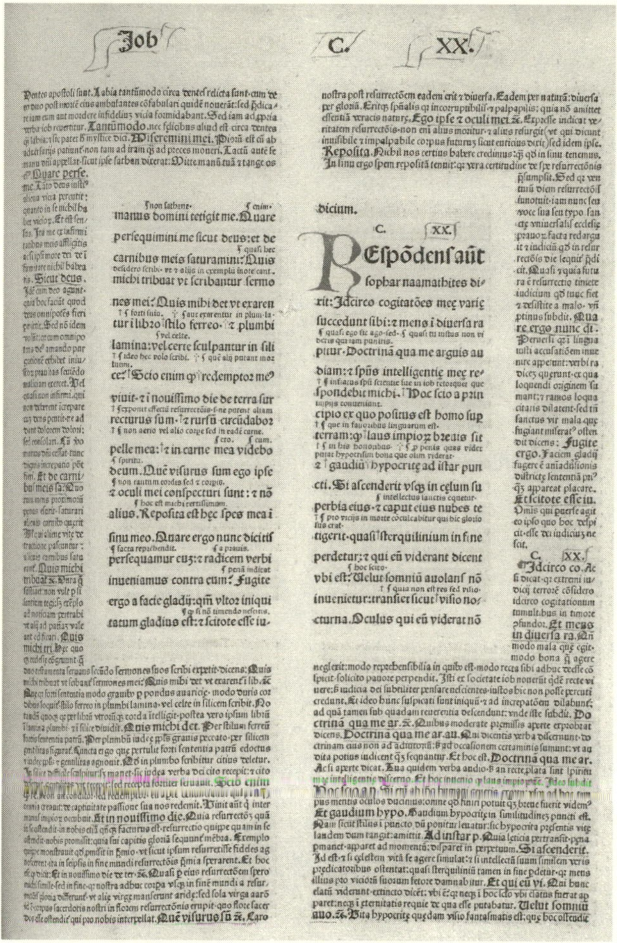

Job C. XX.

manus domini tetigit me. Quare persequimini me sicut deus: et de carnibus meis saturamini? Quis michi tribuat ut scribantur sermones mei? Quis mihi det ut exarentur in libro stilo ferreo et plumbi lamina: vel certe sculpantur in silice? Scio enim quod redemptor meus vivit: et in novissimo die de terra surrecturus sum: et rursum circundabor pelle mea: et in carne mea videbo deum. Quem visurus sum ego ipse et oculi mei conspecturi sunt: et non alius. Reposita est hec spes mea in sinu meo. Quare ergo nunc dicitis persequamur eum: et radicem verbi inveniamus contra eum? Fugite ergo a facie gladii: quoniam ultor iniquitatum gladius est: et scitote esse iudicium.

C. XX.

Respondens autem sophar naamathites dixit: Idcirco cogitationes mee varie succedunt sibi: et mens in diversa rapitur. Doctrinam qua me arguis audiam: et spiritus intelligentie mee respondebit michi. Hoc scio a principio ex quo positus est homo super terram: quod laus impiorum brevis sit et gaudium hypocrite ad instar puncti. Si ascenderit usque in celum superbia eius: et caput eius nubes tetigerit: quasi sterquilinium in fine perdetur: et qui eum viderant dicent ubi est? Velut somnium avolans non invenietur: transiet sicut visio nocturna. Oculus qui eum viderat non

Figure 3. In the medieval *Glossa Ordinaria*—here a sixteenth-century printed version—the biblical text floated like an island in a sea of authorized interpretation. Here we see the end of Chapter 19 and the beginning of 20. Courtesy Firestone Library, Princeton University.

illustrations. Works like the twelfth-century *Bibles Moralisées* and the cycles of stained glass windows they informed paired images of Old Testament and New Testament scenes, showing the way every Christian was to understand the Old Testament. Arguably these images illustrate the play of type and antitype that defined the way medieval Christians viewed the Bible more directly than textual commentaries can. The claims being made were not about words. Through typological anticipation God wrote in events and scenes. To see the same structure, the same postures of different bodies, in scenes paired in this way is to understand how divine purpose wove through events. It was not necessary for the faithful to be able to read written language to understand the way God wrote history.

The larger structure of history and saving knowledge was made clear in a different way in the fifteenth-century works known as Bibles of the poor, *Biblia Pauperum*. Here scenes from the life of Christ (mainly his miracles and passion) are presented in sequence, each in an elaborate architectural frame. Appearing on either side, like buttresses holding up a gothic church nave, are typologically related Old Testament scenes. Supporting text scrolls from pairs of prophets unfurl above and below, so the New Testament scene is framed by six allegorical, typological, or prophetic anticipations.

Figure 4. The *Biblia pauperum* (Bible of the poor) represented the relationship of Old to New Testament architecturally. Old Testament scenes were taken out of the context of their own stories to support New Testament interpretation. Job's children are feasting at left. Courtesy Firestone Library, Princeton University.

The only significant blocks of text decode the two Old Testament scenes depicted.

The correlations are anything but straightforward. On one page, celebrating the feast awaiting the resurrected, we see Job's children feasting as a support to an image of Christ gathering the blessed in his mantel (see figure 4). The accompanying text explains:

> We read in the Book of Job, chapter 1[:5], that Job's sons after sending for their sisters so they could eat and drink with them held a feast in each of their homes. The sons of Job are the holy ones who held feasts daily, sending for those who were to be saved so they could come to eternal joy and enjoy God forever, amen.[6]

That Job's children are killed in the middle of one of their daily feasts just a few verses later (1:19) is beside the point; this is an image of heaven. Refracted in the light of the gospel, however, this may be irrelevant. What was important may simply have been that Job's sons numbered seven and their sisters three (significant numbers both), and that they held feasts daily. But we shouldn't suppose readers weren't familiar with the story of Job, which could add further shadings of meaning. Job 1:5 also tells us that Job "offer[ed] burnt-offerings" for his children, thinking "'It may be that my children have sinned, and cursed God in their hearts." Perhaps "Everyman"-like reflection was called for? The central panel, referring to the story of Dives and Lazarus (Luke 16:22), doesn't portend well for feasters, either.

Despite the idea of *sola scriptura*, the printed Bibles of the Reformers didn't immediately dispense with glosses, or with illustrations. Editions of Martin Luther's German Bible soon included an already stock image conflating a number of scenes from Job (see figure 5). Messengers bring news of the calamities we see in the background behind them—fire from heaven, camel abduction, and the collapsed house of Job's sons—to a Job who is already afflicted with sores and attended by friends— friends whose gazes mirror the flames above them. (The youngest, Elihu, seems to be speaking.) Job's wife remonstrates from the side, her profile continuous with the destruction above her. In later iterations of this image, storm clouds are brewing overhead; in some, Job is illuminated by a beam of light coming from an opening in the clouds, making every part of the story simultaneous.

It is not only for reasons of economy that such illustrations present all that happens in Job's story at once. The Bible doesn't merely narrate a history—a series of events whose meaning lies only in their place in the sequence. Each element is significant

Job in the Ancient Interpreters 37

Figure 5. Martin Luther's German Bible was not the first
vernacular translation of the Christian Bible, but it marked
a sea change in public access to scripture. The engraving that
accompanied the translation of the book of Job in this first
complete edition of Old and New Testaments (1536) brings
together many parts of the story in one image. Courtesy Firestone Library, Princeton University.

on its own and potentially relevant at any time. Different parts may be relevant simultaneously. A composite image, which the eye can take in at a single glance or navigate in endlessly different ways, gives us a better picture of how a familiar narrative like Job's was experienced. In this world, prosperity is always haunted by calamity, just as tragedy is attended by hope. Even if Job passed through the storm only once, for the faithful encountering his story over and over—as text, and in their own lives—he may seem to be spinning in it still, just as we are.

The allegorical realms of the *Glossa* have lost their sway, but Bibles full of clarification and commentary continue to shape the way we understand the book of Job. Even among literalist Protestants who allow no extra-biblical sources for interpretation, the Bible has been mined to reveal a dense network of internal references and clarifications (see figure 10). Texts like the *Jewish Study Bible* balance the best modern translation with interpretive suggestions based on philological work of medieval and modern provenance, suggesting that passages might (or might not) benefit from reordering (see figure 9). And the book of Job continues to reach new readerships, as Christian missionary translation programs reach out to hundreds of languages, and engage new worlds of signification (see figure 11).

Filling Gaps

The book of Job as we know it today seems to speak out of both sides of its mouth. Job helps God win a wager by not cursing him, and then comes very close to cursing God. After being challenged by God for speaking without knowledge, Job is vindicated by God for having spoken rightly. To confuse things further, the final outcome of Job's story looks a lot like that which the friends (condemned for not having spoken rightly) predicted: recant and you will be restored. In the middle of it all, Job speaks with great wisdom about the unattainability of wisdom, a wisdom he otherwise complains of not finding.

Such tensions as these have been deeply unsettling for pious readers in the past, who did not have the recourse modern readers do of seeing the text as composite or even corrupted. Premodern readers did, however, have resources that we have lost, or are loath to use. Notably, they had multiple versions of the story of Job. Like Sophocles' telling of the story of Antigone, the canonical version was only one of many in circulation. It changes things quite a bit to see the canonical Job not as *the* source, the original impugned or misunderstood by later interpreters, but rather as one voice among others competing to define Job and the significance of his story. The canonical book of Job may well have been the most important source on Job, but it was not the only one. The Bible itself offers training in juggling multiple versions of a story. There are two versions of much of Genesis and Exodus and several creation narratives. Christians canonized four of the gospels circulating in the early centuries of the Common Era.

I've mentioned that the Septuagint is the only significant scriptural variant. A few of its departures from the canonical text have an analog— perhaps a source—in an apocryphal work called the *Testament of Job*. This work seems to have originated among an ascetic and ecstatic Egyptian movement called the Therapeutae, but it is difficult to say which came first. The version of the *Testament of Job* we know could date from any time from the second century BCE to the second century CE, and it may not have been the first. These versions of the Job story, along with Targum found among the Dead Sea Scrolls and the Peshitta, are more like each other than like the canonical text. It seems probable that it was this tradition, rather than the canonical text, to which the epistle of James refers when it assumes its readers will have "heard of the patience of Job" (5:1). While the term "patience" doesn't even appear in the canonical text, the patriarch of the *Testament of Job* tells the children assembled at his deathbed that "patience is better than anything" (XVII, 634).[7]

The story of the *Testament of Job* at first seems to be from a parallel universe. Yet, if we listen closely, we can hear challenges to the canonical story, even where the *Testament of Job* may seek to avoid them. Tracking these differences shows which parts of the canonical text were considered problematic by the community that produced and preserved the *Testament of Job*. Significantly, however, most of the aspects of the canonical story the *Testament of Job* seems to want to eliminate are merely displaced, reappearing in different places within the story.

The hero of this story is Jobab, king of all Egypt. *Hassatan* is clearly Satan. God has become a more remote character, speaking through intermediaries. The role of Job's wife is enlarged, the dialogue between Job and his friends abbreviated. The most significant difference from the canonical book is the very different cognitive situation in which the *Testament of Job*'s protagonist finds himself. Jobab knows exactly what will happen to him. Indeed, he knowingly brings it on himself. After wondering if a "much-venerated idol's temple . . . [c]an really be [to] the God who made the heaven and the earth and the sea" (II, 622), he learns in a dream that it is indeed a shrine to the devil. Incensed, Jobab asks permission to destroy it (III, 623).

> And the light answered me and said, You can indeed cleanse this sanctuary, but ... [Satan] will turn against you in anger and fight against you; but although he will afflict you with many calamities, he will not be able to kill you. He will take your possessions away; he will destroy your children. But if you endure, I will make your name famous among all generations on earth until the end of time. And I will return your possessions to you, and double shall be restored to you ... And you will be raised up at the resurrection. (IV, 623)

Jobab razes the temple, and the predicted afflictions arrive—once Satan secures the permission to visit them upon him (VIII, 624–25). The ensuing torments are described in far greater detail and take much longer than seems to be implied in the canonical book, but this allows for a description of Jobab's prodigiously virtuous life. His charity was so extensive that his slaves grew weary and "call[ed] down curses" on him (XIII, 627). When "my slave girls started complaining," he recounts, "I would take the harp out and sing of the wages of recompense; and I would put an end to their fault-finding and complaints" (XIV, 627).

When Satan comes and destroys his goods, seven years later, Jobab is unperturbed: "The Lord gave, the Lord has taken away" (XIX, 630). He's similarly stoic when Satan afflicts him with disease and with worms. "[I]f ever a worm crawled out, I would pick it up and put it back in the same place, saying, Stay in the same place where you were put, till instruction is given by him who gave you your orders" (XX, 630). This goes on for forty-eight years, during which Jobab is supported by his wife Sitidos, whose humiliating labors and begging are described in detail.

Finally, Satan tricks Sitidos into selling her hair for bread, and her heart is led astray. In an eloquent speech similar to that in the Septuagint, she declares herself unable to go on. Jobab knows her words to be the work of the devil, but they still leave him more "dispirited" than anything he has so far suffered, and he tries to rally her:

> This is a burden we both of us bear together—
> the loss of our children and possessions: would
> you have us now curse the Lord and so de-
> prive ourselves of the great wealth that is to
> be? Why is it you do not remember the great
> benefits we once enjoyed? If, then, we have re-
> ceived good at the Lord's hand, should we not
> also endure evil? But let us be patient till the

Lord is moved with pity and shows us mercy.
(XXVI, 633)

He calls to Satan, whom he knows to be behind
Sitidos, and Satan concedes defeat. "Lo, Job[ab], I
am exhausted, and I give in to you, though you are
human and I am a spirit" (XXVII, 634). In time,
four "neighboring kings" come, Elihu among them.
Elihu laments Jobab's fall from grace and the other
kings make similar noises until Jobab bids them
be silent: his true throne is not an earthly one but
"among the saints." The theodicy question is posed
not by Jobab but by Bildad: "Who took away your
possessions and brought these misfortunes on
you? . . . *Was he not unjust (it is for you to judge)* in
bringing these misfortunes on you . . . ? If he gave
and took away, he ought not to have given anything
at all . . . Or should we presume to attribute injustice
to the Lord?" (XXXVII, 639). But Jobab will have
none of it.

Eventually Sitidos returns and dies happy, having seen her children safe in heaven; the whole
city mourns her, even its animals (XL, 641). After
twenty-seven days, Elihu attacks Jobab's character,
and is exposed as the mouthpiece of Satan by God
himself. God's speeches are not reported here, but
all the kings hear them. Eliphaz, Bildad, and Zophar are given a chance to make amends, "for you

were wrong in what you said about my servant Job[ab]" (XLII, 642). Elihu is not forgiven, and Eliphaz denounces him in song (XLIII). All is restored; Jobab starts a new family with a new wife, Jacob's daughter Dinah.

As he prepares to die, Jobab assembles his new family and divides up his estate. His daughters receive magical "cords of many colors" which allow them to speak in tongues (XLVI, 645). Jobab explains that he received them from God when he called him to "gird his loins like a man" (they also instantly healed his sickness) and "spoke to me in power, showing me what has been and what will be" (XLVII, 645), as well as musical instruments, with which the daughters will accompany his body to burial after "he who sat in the great chariot got out and greeted Job[ab]" and took his soul (LII, 647).

Testament of Job is compelling in quite a different way from the canonical book of Job. The canonical story, or some version of it, is presupposed. There are many allusions to it, and some of its most important elements—most notably the divine speeches— are merely summarized. But *Testament's* colorful details and named characters answer many questions raised by the canonical story. Why did Satan attack Job? How was Job able to endure the trials, and how do we know that Satan was defeated? How did Job survive from day to day after the loss of his worldly goods? Did not his wife, too, suffer, and could she have borne ten more children? Who was Elihu? When and how was Job healed of his wounds? Could God really have instigated the whole thing?

But more than details have changed. The patience that the *Testament*'s Jobab commends to his wife and children involves suffering foreseen— indeed calculated—afflictions until a promised release arrives, not suffering affliction whose source, purpose, and end are unknown. Grounded in certain foreknowledge, this patience is more like endurance than faith or hope. The virtue the canonical Job is thought to exemplify requires a cognitive gap. For modern readers, the true challenge of the book of Job is the suffering of the innocent, a suffering whose purpose is never explained to them. As Robert Frost put it in his own amended retelling, Job's affliction "had to seem unmeaning to have meaning."[8] The modern reader notices that one character in the *Testament of Job* does suffer truly Job-like affliction: long-suffering Sitidos has not been told what's going on, and has certainly not chosen her fate.

The figure of the canonical Job, abandoned (for all he knew) by his God, haunts the legend of Job in other ways too. In the canonical book, Job's suffering is defined by its opacity. As the exchanges with his friends make evident, he cannot understand what is happening at all. On closer inspection, much of his pain survives in the *Testament of Job*, though displaced. Canonical Job's situation appears in the speech of *Testament*'s Bildad. His complaints leak out from every mouth but Jobab's, perhaps most interestingly from his servants and slaves, groaning under the demands of a too charitable master. Particularly notable is the displacement of the canonical Job's complaint onto women, from Sitidos to the slave girls (who get a sort of theophany from their master). Even the new improved daughters grumble at their magical cords, perhaps recalling how their biblical counterparts shared in Job's inheritance with their brothers (XLVI, 645).

Testament of Job was among the texts removed from the Apocrypha by Pope Gelasius in the fifth century CE but it evidently lived on: someone thought it important enough to produce the tenth-century copy that is the earliest surviving manuscript. It remains our fullest exposition of the legend of Job. Many of the details that set it apart from the canonical book are constants in the iconographic tradition of Job, from the royal status of Job and his friends to his experience with worms on a dung heap. Oral traditions are notoriously difficult to document, but they have more staying power than is often supposed. The traditions of enactment to which we turn in chapter 3 confirm that the legend of Job endured at least into the early modern period.

It is tempting to dismiss the *Testament of Job* and the tradition of legends of which it formed a part as bowdlerizations of the canonical story, refusals to face its challenges. It may be better to see it as part of a tradition made the richer for giving voice to confidence as well as doubt, assent as well as protest. Indeed, *Testament*'s Jobab and Sitidos stand in a tension akin to that between the Job of the canonical book's prose frame and the Job at its poetic center. It may be that the "patience" Job exemplifies is so difficult to characterize that it requires not just a narrative but the gap between two complementary but contrasting narratives, one of knowledge and one of its absence.

Turning

The *Testament of Job* is a kind of midrash, a retelling of a biblical story which fills in every missing detail (large parts of it are incorporated into Louis Ginzberg's *Legends of the Jews*.[9]) But the experience of Job in the larger corpus of the Talmud is fuller still. More than one answer is given to any question, and more questions are discovered than one might have thought possible. Newly discovered questions are not occasions for consternation, however, but for delight, confirming that the Bible can be turned and turned infinitely.

Its revealed status and continued salience are confirmed by what James Kugel has called its "omnisignificance."[10]

Kugel has argued that the Bible as we know it was the work of "ancient interpreters," both Jewish and later Christian, who, starting after the Babylonian exile, treated their received texts in a new way. Kugel describes four defining assumptions of their approach:

1. They assumed that the Bible was a fundamentally cryptic text: that is, when it said A, it often really meant B. . . .

2. Interpreters also assumed that the Bible was a book of lessons directed to readers in their own day. It may seem to talk about the past, but it is not fundamentally history. It is instruction, telling us what to do . . .

3. Interpreters also assumed that the Bible contained no contradictions or mistakes. . . .

4. Lastly, they believed that the entire Bible is essentially a divinely given text, a book in which God speaks directly or through His prophets.[11]

These assumptions are what "made the Bible the Bible." They explain its enduring status, but also suggest reasons why faith in clear rather than cryptic meaning has made modern biblical interpretation so brittle.

Approaching the Bible as "cryptic, relevant, perfect and divinely granted" challenged interpreters to go through the text with a fine-tooth comb. Noticing an incongruity or opacity or a repetition—the sort of thing that makes a contemporary reader suspect scribal error or intervention—was good news, not bad: there is more to know. Meaning did not perch on the surface of texts, but played hide and seek with readers. The answer to any question raised in and by the Bible could be and must be found in the Bible too—but there was no presumption that the answer would appear in the same part of it. There is a playful virtuosity to many midrashim where an apparently insignificant and unrelated turn of phrase from another book is brought in like the unexpected inheritance that saves the poor protagonist of a Victorian novel.

For these reasons, the fate of the book of Job in midrash can only be gestured at here. Job's person and story were the object of often critical scrutiny—the main object of the discussion that follows—but his words and his story pop up in many places. The poetic sections of Job are a mine of precious stones inlaid in the interpretation of other texts. Some of Job's bitterest words are quoted in the context of the story of Jacob, for instance. As a contemporary midrashist puts it, "Jacob ventriloquized Job's cry of long suffering, which expresses an essential motif of his own life."[12] Job's words of despair or of offense are not his alone but belong to the Bible as a whole, and to those whose lives are grounded in it.

Every detail of the Bible had significance, starting with proper names but also including even homonyms—the multiple meanings a Hebrew term can have if differently vocalized—and even what happened if one letter in a word was changed or the order of two letters inverted (see figure 6). The word read "tempest" could also mean "hair," for instance, and in one midrash we will see, God speaks to Job from *both*. The one thing not sought

Figure 6. (*facing page*). The Leningrad Codex of 1000 CE is the oldest surviving complete Hebrew Bible scripture. This page shows Chapter 13, whose 15th verse has radically different meaning as written (*ketiv*) and read aloud (*qere*). Vowels are not usually marked, but 13:15 is occasion for a rare editorial insertion of a character to ensure that the *qere* meaning prevails. Most contemporary English translations render the *ketiv* ("See, he will kill me, I have no hope"), but the *qere* remains known as one of the most famous lines of the book ("Though he slay me yet will I trust in him" in the King James Version). The Masoretes' *ketiv-qere* here has antecedents in the Targum, the Syriac Peshitta, and the Vulgate. Photograph by Bruce and Kenneth Zuckerman, West Semitic Research, in collaboration with the Ancient Biblical Manuscript Center. Courtesy Russian National Library (Saltykov-Shchedrin).

was closure. If a passage could be understood in several ways, it should be so understood.

Discussions of the figure of Job appear scattered throughout the Talmud. There is no agreement on his status. Some interpreters placed Job in a select group of "god-fearing" men, along with Abraham and Joseph and perhaps Obadiah,[13] and declared him the most pious of gentiles.[14] Others accused Job of considering himself greater than Adam, Abraham, and Moses, who suffered worse afflictions than he (cases of apparent divine arbitrariness

and overreaction are mentioned: Gen 15:13, Num 20:10), but did so without complaint.[15]

In one striking retelling, Job is brought in to answer a knot of problems in the story of Exodus, starting with how the Israelites were able to escape Pharaoh's pursuing army.

It can be compared to a shepherd who was lead-ing his sheep across a river when a wolf came to attack the sheep. . . . He took a large he-goat and threw it to the wolf, saying to himself, "Let him struggle with this until we cross the river, and then I will return and bring him back." So when Israel departed from Egypt, the angel Sa-mael rose to accuse them, pleading before God, "Lord of the universe! Until now they have been worshipping idols, and now You divide the sea for them?" . . . He [God] delivered into his [Samael's] hands Job, one of the counselors of Pharaoh, of whom it is written, "And that man was whole-hearted and upright" (Job 1:1), and said, " 'Behold, he is in your hands' (Job 2:6). While Samael is busily occupied with Job, Israel will go through the sea! Afterwards, I will deliver Job." This is why Job said, "I was at ease, and he broke me asunder." (Job 16:12)[16]

This story offers answers to questions big and small. How were the Israelites able to escape from Egypt?

Who were Pharaoh's counselors (Exod. 7:11)? Job-related questions are answered, too. Who was Job, and when did he live? Why did God single him out for Satan's attentions? In an oblique way, identifying Job as Pharaoh's third, noncommittal, counselor reflects one of the other challenges of Job, who finds his way into the holy books of Israel but seems unrelated to their history and revelation.

The most sustained attention to Job appears in Baba Bathra, part of the Babylonian Talmud ostensibly dedicated to questions of property tort law.[17] Here too there is no default interpretation of Job and his significance. The joints of the story are made looser, not tighter, as the story of Job is retold to address open questions. The Job who appears here can be startlingly different from the canonical figure.

> There was a certain pious man among the heathen named Job, but he [thought that he had] come into this world only to receive his reward [here], and when the Holy One, blessed be He, brought chastisements upon him, he began to curse and blaspheme, so the Holy One, blessed be He, doubled his reward in this world so as to expel him from the world to come. (15b, 75)

This worldly schemer may seem more remote from the canonical Job than the *Testament of Job*, but real questions are deftly answered here. Did not Job curse? Did he not reject a future life? On the other hand, was he not commended by God, and indeed, restored twice what he had lost? This last was particularly troubling as double restoration could be taken to be an admission of culpability. That Job's restoration was not reward but punishment by way of a payoff is the sort of inversion in which midrashic interpretation glories.

The question of Job's identity was in fact a central concern of the rabbis. As we have seen also in the Septuagint and the *Testament of Job*, efforts were made to find his place in the genealogy of Israel. Was Job really not an Israelite? And where on earth was Uz? The Baba Bathra reports but dismisses the claim, made on the basis of one word, that Job must have been a contemporary of Moses; on the basis of one word one may just as easily claim him the contemporary of Isaac, Jacob, or Joseph (15a, 73). Baba Bathra suggests more convincing arguments could be made for Job's being of the generation that returned from the Babylonian exile, although other details in the text suggest the time of spies, the judging of judges, Ahasuerus, the kingdoms of Sheba or the Chaldeans or—since he was thought to have married Dinah—of Jacob (15b, 75–76). In all of these cases but the last, the compiler notes, Job would have to have been an Israelite— for Moses was granted his dying request that the

Divine Presence henceforth appear only to Israelites (15b, 76).

That there was none as righteous and upright as
Job could be a problem if he was a gentile—unless
he was just a fable. Baba Bathra includes the argument of "a certain Rabbi . . . sitting before R. Samuel b. Nahmani" who "in the course of his exposi-
tions remarked, Job never was and never existed,
but is only a typical figure." His interlocutor is un-
impressed. A character in a fable wouldn't have a
specific name and come from a specific country. In
reply the unnamed rabbi appeals to the parable Na-
than tells David at 2 Sam. 12:3, "The poor man had
nothing but one ewe lamb, which he had bought
and nourished up etc." which begins with the same
words as Job and a similarly exaggerated counting
of sheep (15a, 74). As we will see in chapter 2, the
great medieval philosopher Maimonides will take
up the claim that Job is a parable: cases like Job's
"always exist [and] all reflecting people become perplexed." And the tables can be turned on the supposed proper name of Uz, for the "equivocal word
Uz" is "the imperative of a verb meaning to reflect
and meditate . . . It is as if [Scripture] said to you:
Meditate and reflect on this parable. . . ."[18]

Much of the midrash on Job in Baba Bathra cir-
cles around the question of how virtuous and faithful Job really was, especially in comparison with

Job in the Ancient Interpreters   57

Abraham, father of the people of Israel. Abraham generally prevails, but Rabbi Joḥanan found Job worthier of praise than the patriarch (15b, 77). Indeed, it seemed that Job was the favorite of God, since he "gave to Job a taste of the future world." This taste was ingeniously tucked away in Job 1:14—"the oxen were plowing and the asses were eating beside them"—whose suggestion that the times of sowing and reaping were one, Rabbi Joḥanan reasoned, surely signified the future world where conception and birth were one (15b–16a, 77–78). Various aspects of the *Testament of Job*, starting with Jobab's responding to the angel "Here am I" (III, 622), can be understood in connection with discussion of the priority of Job versus Abraham.

Baba Bathra's compiler frames these ideas with a retelling of the scenes in the heavenly court, scenes that beg for explanation. God asks the satan to look around on earth, who duly reports, "Sovereign of the Universe, I have traversed the whole world and found none so faithful as thy servant Abraham" (15b, 76–77). God asks him to consider Job. A second time, God sends him to scan the world. A second time, the satan comes back praising Abraham. A second time God directs his attention to Job, who persists in his integrity: "although thou [Satan] movedst me against him to destroy him without cause [2:3]." Rabbi Joḥanan is quoted again. "Were it not expressly stated in the Scripture, we would not dare to say it. [God is made to appear] like a man who allows himself to be persuaded against his better judgment" (16a, 78). But who is this satan anyway? "Resh Lakish said: Satan, the evil prompter, and the Angel of Death are all one" (16a, 79), but this doesn't mean he is only or even primarily a force for evil. Rabbi Levi finds he had a "pious purpose" in acting as adversary: "Satan, when he saw God inclined to favor Job said, Far be it that God should forget the love of Abraham" (16a, 79).

Job may have been the apple of God's eye before the satan got to work, but it's clear to most of the rabbis that the man from Uz didn't pass the test. Could there be clearer evidence than the shift from 1:22 ("In all this Job did not sin or charge God with wrongdoing") to 2:10 ("In all this Job did not sin with his lips")? Raba thought it obvious that Job sinned in his heart. Soon he sinned with his lips, too. In 9:24 ("The earth is given into the hand of the wicked: he covers the eyes of its judges— if it is not he, who then is it?") and elsewhere, Raba complained, "Job sought to turn the dish upside down." Abaye defended Job, but the same issue came up later between Rabbis Eliazar and Joshua (16a, 79); the issue is clearly not settled. Job denied free will at 10:7, seeking to exculpate the whole world at God's expense, and fully merited Eliphaz' reproof at 15:4

("you are doing away with the fear of God, and hindering meditation before God"). Rab said, "Dust should be put in the mouth of Job" for making himself a colleague of God (6:2) and for arguing with his master (9:33) (16a, 80). However, Rab found Job's words mitigated by his suffering (16b, 82).

Baba Bathra contains a tour-de-force refutation— not attributed to any particular sage—of the view that God is unfair to Job and ignores his pleas for explanation. This passage is worth quoting at length, for it shines a light not only on the world of Job but also on the world of midrash. The argument rests on the close resemblance of the words Job [*Iyob*] and enemy [*Oyeb*]. (Job accuses God of taking him for his enemy at 13:24 and 33:10.)

> Job said to God: Perhaps a tempest has passed before thee, and caused thee to confuse *Iyob* and *Oyeb*. He was answered through a tempest, as it is written, *Then the Lord answered Job out of the whirlwind and said, ... Gird up now thy loins like a man, for I will demand of thee and declare thou unto me.* [38:1, 3] I have created many hairs in man, and for every hair I have created a separate groove, so that two should not suck from the same groove, for if two were to suck from the same groove they would impair the sight of a man. I do not confuse one groove

with another; and shall I then confuse *Iyob* with *Oyeb*? *Who hath cleft a channel for the water-flood?* [38:25] Many drops have I created in the clouds, and for every drop a separate mould, so that two drops should not issue from the same mould, since if two drops issued from the same mould they would wash away the soil, and it would not produce fruit. I do not confuse one drop with another, and shall I confuse *Iyob* and *Oyeb*? ... *Knowest thou the time when the wild goats of the rock bring forth, or canst thou mark when the hinds do calve?* [39:1] This wild goat is heartless towards her young. When she crouches for delivery, she goes up to the top of a mountain so that the young shall fall down and be killed, and I prepare an eagle to catch it in his wings and set it before her, and if he were one second too soon or too late it would be killed. I do not confuse one moment with another, and shall I confuse *Iyob* with *Oyeb*? (16a–b, 81)

The image of a God attentive to the smallest detail, engaged with the welfare of each individual thing in nature, no matter how tiny, is a powerful one. God's discussions of meteorological and zoological terrors are glossed here as remarkably provident uses of apparent evils to serve good. Striking, too, is the suggestion that it's all about reading. God hasn't *misread* Job's name, his place in the text of creation. His prodigious and meticulous care of his creation is like the rabbis' virtuosic care for the texts of scripture—including seemingly heartless ones like the book of Job. And all of this starts in the recognition that *se'arah* means both "tempest" and "hair."

The book of Job's linguistic treasures show up throughout the midrash, but Job himself was not an important model. Others enjoyed divine favor, as well as divine attention of a more painful sort but bore the test better. Job's complaints, which will make him a paragon to moderns, were not held up as exemplary. Indeed, nothing about him was exemplary. In Leviticus Rabbah's discussion of unintentional sin (Lev. 4:5–6), Job's questioning is seen as dangerous:

> It is said, *Shall one man sin, and wilt Thou be wroth will all the congregation?* (Num. XVI, 22). R. Simeon b. Yohai taught: This may be compared to the case of men on a ship, one of whom took a borer and began boring beneath his own place. His fellow travellers said to him: "What are you doing?" Said he to them: "What does that matter to you, am I not boring under my own place?" Said they: "Because the water will come up and flood the ship for us all." Even so did Job say, *And be it indeed that I have erred, mine error remaineth with myself* (Job XIX, 4),

and his friends said, *He adds transgression unto his sin, he extends it among us.*[19]

That Job was not an example to be followed is confirmed by his exclusion from the emerging liturgy. Job may be good for thinking, but he is distracting to practice.

Reading the book of Job through the midrash reminds us of the text's wealth of interpretive openings and opportunities, including many we might not otherwise have noticed. The book of Job was decoded with reference to the whole of scripture, and its words and scenarios were available for unlocking meanings throughout the Bible. In all this discussion, however, Job's own voice can be hard to hear. Midrash's loosening of the hinges of Job's story may seem to obscure its most fundamental challenge. What if Job's complaints against God were not just expressions of weakness of character or the loss of self-control, which pain and catastrophic loss might produce in the best of men? What if he was raising unanswerable questions about the justice of God?

Threshing

Early Christian interpreters of the book of Job were playing much the same game as their Jewish contemporaries. Like Kugel's other "ancient inter-preters," they assumed that the Bible was speaking to them, that it was perfect and complete, that it was entirely consistent with itself, and that it often concealed its most important messages. Apparent contradiction, redundancy, or absurdity were in-vitations to dig deeper and read more broadly and creatively. The biblical text raises questions large and small and yields answers to them all.

While the game and its rules were the same, however, the universe of scripture mined and re-combined was of course different. The New Testa-ment was taken to be the key to the Old Testament, which pointed mutely beyond itself, through typol-ogy, toward Christ. Old Testament narratives had to be shown to be incomplete in their own terms, but completed by the life and teaching of Christ. A smug Christian looking at the midrash-spinning rabbis would have concluded that their unending virtuosity confirmed the insufficiency of the He-brew scriptures to interpret themselves. Had not Saint Paul asserted that a "veil" lay over the minds of the Jews in reading the Torah, a veil removed only "when one turns to the Lord [Jesus]" (2 Cor. 3:16)? On the other hand, the Old Testament was needed for a full understanding of the New.

Christ shone through every crack in the Old Testament. The work of making the New and Old

Testaments indispensable to each other involved a kind of interpretation going back to the school of Alexandria, focused on the multiple "senses" of scripture. The "literal" or "historical" sense—what the words actually say—was distinguished from additional "spiritual" senses, which reveal the text (also) to be about other things. The "moral" sense seeks models for conduct. The "allegorical" reads every line as potentially revealing something about Christ or the Church. The "anagogical" sense derives insights into the journey of the soul. In the process, the historical meaning could be not merely deepened but overthrown.

The book of Job had a particularly important place in Christian exegesis. Job was a prophetic figure who knew of the coming of Christ.[20] He was seen also as prefiguring Christ's innocent suffering. In both these capacities, he became a significant figure in Christian liturgy and life. Indeed, as a gentile, righteous and recognized as such by God, Job was a sort of Christian *avant la lettre*.

While all the church fathers engaged with the book of Job, one work on Job became a foundational text of the Christian Middle Ages—Gregory the Great's *Morals in Job*, written between 578 and 595 CE. The author, feeling a personal affinity with Job through a life of unremitting physical pain, found in the book of Job not only a meaning for suffering but a way of weaning oneself from the illusions of fallen existence. In the process, he interwove the rest of the Christian scriptures so tightly with Job that *Morals in Job* became the go-to book not just for those interested in Job, but for anyone seeking to understand the nature of existence in this middle region of sin and suffering. In his revaluation of values, Gregory makes short work of the literal sense of Job. In a revealing image, he invites his readers to "put aside the chaff of the history and to feed on the grain of mysteries" (35.16.36).[21] The chaff is not revalued or recontextualized but turned inside out and then left behind, because whole new orders of meaning and significance have been disclosed.

A good illustration of the fractal fruitfulness of Gregory's method is what he makes of Job's scratching his boils with a potsherd (Job 2:8). Why a potsherd? At the historical level, a potsherd is a broken piece of pottery with a sharp edge. Gregory thinks Job takes up the potsherd not only to relieve his pain but also as a reminder that he, too, is mud—the mud of pottery scratching a son of Adam, made from mud—as well as broken (3.7.9). Job's pious figuring is still at the historical level, but it opens the way to further meanings. At the allegorical level the scraping movement is the same, but it is not Job making it. Christ is doing the scraping—though he is also the potsherd. Christ has taken on the "clay of our nature" (3.17.33), clay which,

having "received firmness by fire" through the Passion, is able to scrape away the mud of sin:

> And so the Mediator between God and man,
> the Man Jesus Christ, in giving up His Body
> into the hands of those who persecuted Him,
> scraped the [pus] with a potsherd, forasmuch
> as He put away sin by flesh; for He came, as it is
> written, in the likeness of sinful flesh, that He
> might condemn sin of sin [Romans 8:3, Vulg].
> And whilst He presented the purity of His own
> Flesh to the enemy, He cleansed away the defile-
> ments of ours. (3.17.33)

In the moral reading, finally, the potsherd represents the "severity" with which we should exam-
ine ourselves, its edge given by its reminder that we
are mortal. "The [pus] is soon cleansed away if the
frailty of our nature be taken up in thought, like a
potsherd in the hand" (3.40.58). A reference to the
strictness of the Sermon on the Mount (Matthew
5:27–28) makes clear what kind of scraping will ensure that "sin is not only severed from the deed, but
also from the thought" (3.30.58).

While Gregory's title is *Morals in Job*, the allegorical sense is crucial. Gregory does not proceed
directly from the historical sense to the moral, and
would not have us try to do so. The Sermon on
the Mount tells us what to do but not how. Only

Christ's taking up the potsherd—offering himself as potsherd—makes the moral attainable for us. Fallen human nature is vile until sin is scraped away, something only the passion-hardened sacrifice of Christ (not just his teachings) can achieve. For Gregory, Job was a prophet who could see past and future.[22] Already in his taking up of the potsherd he prefigured the coming of Christ.

As Gregory scrapes away one layer to disclose another beneath it, he reveals a reality that exists and functions in a radically different way than we commonly assume. The allegorical sense shows the world to be an entirely different kind of place than the historical sense suggests. Allegory isn't just a way of reading *texts*, but a way of reading *things*. The moral sense doesn't primarily show a reader how to be moral in the world described by the historical sense, but how to participate in a reality best described by allegory.

Like the legendary hero of *The Testament of Job*, Gregory's Job is a fighter for God. The *Testament's* Jobab triumphs by enduring. Gregory's Job does not merely endure, but learns through his suffering. He does not learn to be good: he is from the outset, as the biblical text insists (1:1), a blameless and upright man. God wins his bet with Satan, and anyone who thinks otherwise sins. However, Gregory's Job also learns something of surpassing importance along the way. Driven by suffering to look inward,

he sees that everything created is as nothing compared to God.

When he "cursed the day of his birth" (3:1), Gregory's Job condemned the world, not God. Job 3 has always been an interpretive challenge, not least because
Job here comes so close to proving the satan right,
who had wagered: "stretch out your hand now, and
touch his bone and his flesh, and he will curse you
to your face" (2:5, cf. 1:11). In fact, Gregory explains,
Job, his eyes opened by suffering, is merely describing what he now *sees*. Holy men don't curse, certainly
not ones commended by God for having "spoken of
me what is right" (42:7, 8). More significantly, it's not
possible to curse something that doesn't exist—like
the day in the past when you were born. Noticing this
is just what the text wants us to do. The ancient interpreter Gregory reflects that "literal words sometimes
contradict themselves; but whilst by their opposite-
ness they stand at variance with themselves, they direct the reader to a truth that is to be understood"
(4.Praef.1). Once we understand that Job can't be
saying what he seems to be saying, the truth emerges:

For what is to be understood by "the day of
our birth," save the whole period of our mortal
state?... [H]e saith not, "Let the day perish
wherein I was created," but, let the day perish
wherein I was born. For man was created in a

day of righteousness, but now he is born in a
time of guilt; for Adam was created, but Cain
was the first man that was born. What then is it
to curse the day of his birth, but to say plainly,
"May the day of change perish, and the light of
eternity burst forth?" (4.1.4)

The curse in Job 3 turns out not to be a curse at all
but a vivid account of a fallen world whose end
any right-minded person will look forward to with
impatience.

Job has still more to learn. God's two speeches
lay out the essentially military apparatus of the
church, certain to prevail against the massed forces
of Behemoth and Leviathan, figures of Satan and
the Antichrist. On his own, even upright Job would
be helpless. Christ's human nature was the "hook"
on which God caught Leviathan (33.7.14; cf. Job
41:1). The message rings clear. Job must recognize
that, for all his virtue and understanding, he cannot
prevail alone: "what commonly slays a soul more
fatally than consciousness of virtue?" (28.Praef.1).
Satan's power is too great.

The upshot is that the "most dangerous evil in life
is not suffering but tranquility."[23] Lucky are those to
whom God sends the wake-up call of suffering:

[B]ecause in the midst of the divine appoint-
ments the human mind is closed in by the great

darkness of its uncertainty, holy men, when
they see this world's prosperity to be their lot,
are disquieted with fearful misgivings. For they
fear lest they should receive here the fruit of
their labours. They fear lest divine justice should
see in them a secret wound, and in loading them
with external blessings should withhold from
them the interior.... And hence it is that holy
men are in greater dread of prosperity in this
world than of adversity. (5.1.1)

As one recent interpreter has paraphrased it, suffering is to be welcomed as the chemotherapy required to combat the cancer of sin.[24] The problem
of evil is turned on its head. As C. S. Lewis was to
argue in *The Problem of Pain*, the issue is not that
God should leave the wicked untreated, but that he
should not offer treatment for all the virtuous in
need of healing.

To Gregory, Job's and God's words are rich with
allegorical and moral significance. The really interesting interpretive problems come with Job's friends.
Determining what kind of friends they are is the
smaller challenge. For Gregory they are what they
claim to be, friends to Job, concerned to help him reconcile with his God by reminding him of God's glory.
The challenge lies in the fact that their words are
theologically correct. No less an authority than the

apostle Paul quotes from Eliphaz as from a reliable authority (1 Cor. 3:19, citing Job 5:13; 5.11.27, 22.31.35). And yet the friends are reproved by God (42:7).

Eliphaz, Bildad, and Zophar, Gregory declares, are at the historical level friends to Job, trying honestly to console him. If anything they may go too far in their heartfelt grief. There is no flaw in what they say. At the allegorical level, however, they represent heresy (6.1.2, 12.24.30). This is a most disconcerting claim. Gregory does not share modern interpreters' sense that they are false friends. Indeed Job's friends must be appreciated to be true friends at the historical level, if we are to understand all the text is telling us. "[H]eretics have this especial peculiarity, that they mix good and evil, so that they may easily delude the sense of the hearer" (5.11.28), and not all heretics know what they are doing. We ought not to venture out on our own beyond authoritative interpretation either.

It is an alarming thought that a true friend at one level could represent a true foe at another. Yet, Gregory observes, "it very often happens that a circumstance is virtue in the historical fact, evil in its meaning and import, just as an action is sometimes in the doing ground of condemnation, but in the writing, a prophecy of merit" (3.18.55). In case we are not sufficiently upset by the upside-down world Gregory is describing, he turns to one of the

most disturbing episodes where historical vice is allegorical virtue, David's destruction of Uriah in 2
Samuel:

> And whom does Uriah denote, but the Jewish
> people, whose name is rendered by interpre-
> tation, "My light from God?" . . . But David
> took from this Uriah his wife, and united her
> to himself, surely in that the strong-handed
> One, which is the rendering of "David," our
> Redeemer, shewed Himself in the flesh, whilst
> He made known that the Law spake in a spiri-
> tual sense concerning Himself. Hereby, that it
> was held by them after the letter, He proved
> it to be alienated from the Jewish people, and
> joined it to Himself, in that He declared Him-
> self to be proclaimed by it. . . . Uriah is sent to
> Joab with letters, according to which he is to
> be put to death, in that the Jewish people bears
> itself the Law, by whose convicting testimony it
> is to die. . . . What, then, in respect of the fact,
> is more foul than David? What can be named
> purer than Uriah? What again in respect of the
> mystery can be discovered holier than David,
> what more faithless than Uriah? (3.18.55)

The reader is supposed to have a sublime experience
in the savagery of these inversions, and to bring this
to the reading of the book of Job.

Job in the Ancient Interpreters   73

Gregory didn't have to bring up the shocking story of David and Uriah in expounding the morals of Job. He does so *because* it is shocking. Things are not as they seem. The book of Job is a book of necessary violence. It shows that ours is an "inverted world."[25] The historical is not to be trusted, certainly not where it conflicts with the allegorical or moral. The implications of a historical crime disclosing supercessionist virtue spill over beyond allegory. Many of Uriah's people would be killed by Gregory's. The main import, however, was to be internal. The friends, along with Job's wife and other "foolish women," were types for every man's carnal nature. They represented life lived at the merely historical level, rejecting the Christianizing spiritual interpretations revealed and assured by authority. Taught by suffering and the perfidy of his wife and friends, Job "beheld . . . the truth with the eye within," and so "more clearly discerned and beheld the darkness of his humanity" (35.4.5). Penance naturally followed. As Job rightly repented in dust and ashes, so much the more must we all repent.

The world is seriously out of joint, but not fatally or finally so. We must learn to distrust the assurances of our senses. Prosperity is a trap. Friendship can breed heresy. In the end, everything we do is as nothing. Yet threshing out the "historical" chaff of

Job's story shows the way to a glorious restoration. In the end, heretics are welcomed back—at God's stern but forgiving invitation—and even the Jews are welcomed. The sacrifice Job performs for his friends (42:8–9) shows the gravity of their sin. Bulls represent the pride and rams the leaders of heretical groups; Job represents a church that will perform absolution for them (8.Praef. 35.8.12, 14). The arrival of Job's brethren (42:11) represents the conversion of the Jews at the end of this world. Their gifts of sheep are types of "obedience" and "innocence," the "earring of gold" each brings connotes "hearing adorned with the grace of humility" (35.13.26–27). At the moral level, every part of the story was required of each Christian soul.

From the standpoint of modern literary traditions, allegory may seem mere poetry. But for Gregory this poetry discloses the true nature and meaning of a world where the grandeur of God flames out, in the words of poet Gerard Manley Hopkins, "like shining from shook foil." Allegoresis does not add a layer of new meaning to an otherwise self-evident world. It teaches us to see beyond the false certainties of that world to what's really going on. Without this vision we cannot live as we are called to live. From the book of Job, Gregory authoritatively derives this saving knowledge—and learns that this saving knowledge can be truly gained only through suffering, loneliness, cognitive collapse, and penance. Gregory's Job is our guide through these depths and out of them again.

It would be a long time before the voice of the protagonist of the book of Job could rise above the cadences of storytelling, the crystal halls of mi-drashic mirrorings, and the cosmic alchemy of al-legoresis. Contemporary readers may be bemused, if not dismayed, by the history of Job's reception described in this chapter. Instead of just reading the text before them, early Jewish as well as Christian readers added text of their own. If they didn't like what they saw, they turned it upside-down. And unlike many later readings, they attend to every de-tail, but they seem willfully to abandon all sense of proportion, allowing what seem to us minor details to overshadow the central story.

The *Testament of Job*, Baba Bathra, and *Morals in Job* represent three different ways of pulling rab-bits out of the hat of Job. But before we dismiss these ways of reading we should consider that what they're doing is just a more explicit version of what we all do in interpretation. Every story ex-ists in several iterations. Every story has openings that allow different interpretations. And every story is read in terms of other commitments, be-liefs, and expectations. The ancient interpreters' ways of reading might complicate the assumptions framing our understanding of what reading the book of Job involves. The seemingly upside-down world they evoke may disclose to us not only the mysteries of the Bible but the mysterious heart of creation itself.

Job in Disputation

The proliferation of stories swirling around Job described in the last chapter may give us pause. The
eagerness to retell the story seems to suggest a reluc-
tance to let it tell itself and a refusal even to acknowledge its central challenge. Why does God permit an
innocent and virtuous man like Job to suffer? Reasons have been proposed—battling for God against
Satan, testing, purification—but we may still think
them unconvincing. Is it all for Job's benefit? Must
so many others suffer that he might learn? And is
suffering the only way these lessons can be learned?
God seems callous or careless. Whatever is said of the
character of Job, are not more unsettling questions
raised about the character of God? Experiences like
Job's raise a classic philosophical problem:

> Epicurus' old questions are yet unanswered.
> Is [God] willing to prevent evil, but not able?

then is he impotent. Is he able, but not willing?
then is he malevolent. Is he both able and willing? whence then is evil?[1]

This chapter looks at interpretations of the book
of Job concerned with this philosophical problem,
indeed as itself fundamentally a philosophical discussion of divine justice, evil, and human experience. These interpreters are not hostile to allegorical and other ways of figuring the text, but theirs is
a distinct project. What room does the book of Job
define or allow for human understanding of divine
providence?

The readings of Job and evil we explore in this
chapter are different from the modern way of interpreting Epicurus' questions, which has been
described as the "atheistic problem of evil"[2]—
essentially, "God or evil?" We'll explore the emergence of that question in chapter 4. Here we encounter traditions that engage the same questions
yet go in different directions. They might regard
modern questioning as one-sided. The question
"if . . . there be a God, from whence proceed so
many evils?" is posed in Boethius' *Consolation of
Philosophy*, written in the early sixth century, but is
only half the problem. It continues: "and if there be
no God, from whence cometh any good?"[3] Much
premodern reflection on the problem of evil was

connected to reflection also on the nature of good, indeed of substance itself, both of which were unimaginable without God.

These thinkers could not imagine reason's deposing God, and thought at least the natural world too well ordered to be the work of chance. Yet most also accepted—even insisted—that, on the face of it, the world of human experience did not look like the work of a good and powerful God. The problem was approached not atheistically but "aporetically, as generating a puzzle."[4] The book of Job raises questions less about the existence of God than about his nature. Philosophical dilemmas like the ones posed by Epicurus allow for no easy solution, and so force us to deepen our understanding of the substance of all experience and of the attributes of God. There are continuities between this approach to problems of philosophical theology and the approach to texts of the ancient interpreters, inspired by apparent problems in the text to ever more playful and powerful interpretations.

If the existence of God is given, the issue becomes one of the status of philosophy. None of the foundational figures for Jewish, Catholic, and Protestant traditions explored in this chapter ventures a theodicy, a "justification of the ways of God to men."[5] Divine transcendence precludes and prevents that. What could humanly comprehensible

CHAPTER 2

concepts hope to understand of creation, let alone of the creator? The book of Job was seen by many as a crucial overture from the divine, a lesson about what human beings might nevertheless grasp of providence, and how. It was also an account of how such issues could and should be discussed. The book of Job was not just a dramatization of philosophical arguments. It showed how—and how not—to engage in philosophical discussion on providence in the first place.

Instead of telling back stories or parallel stories about Job and generally uninterested in who Job really was, these readings approached the book of Job as philosophy. Six-sevenths of the book is given over to argumentation if you include Elihu—and still more if God is seen as making an argument, too. The characters in the book of Job are read as representations of important philosophical arguments about providence. The progress of the exchanges makes Job's friends' general arguments subside into shrilly *ad hominem* attacks, of course, while Job's personal confusion takes on a progressively more general tone. These transformations are instructive about the nature and limits of disputation.

The exchanges of Job with his friends are not happy ones that lead to mutual discoveries and appreciations, let alone convergence. Part of the story of the book of Job is this breakdown of

conversation. In order for the breakdown to be significant, however, the discussion has to start legitimately, among friends. Medieval readers, Jewish as
well as Christian, understood the book of Job to
be describing a friendship of philosophers. There
are clearly perils to disputation, especially perhaps
to disputations about providence and disputations
about individual cases. Job and his friends become
angry at each other, and God becomes angry at the
friends. But Job and his friends are reconciled at the
end, at God's command. Job's restoration follows
not on anything he said before or after God spoke,
but on his praying for the friends who have abused
him (42:10).

It takes more than a little ingenuity to read
Job as the transcript of an actual or even a mythi-
cal conversation, but such interpretations take the
actual shape and dynamics of the book of Job seriously. Interpreters' efforts to understand the book's
speeches as part of a debate lead them to ever more
careful parsing of the text's literal meaning. If the
anguish eddying around some of Job's words can get
lost in these analyses, his voice is sounding louder
and more clearly than in the versions of the ancient
interpreters. The interpersonal context of meaning-
making is brought into sharp focus—especially
through a detailed understanding of when and
how it breaks down. Some kinds of philosophical

engagement take a beating, but the value of careful argument, caution in application of general
thoughts to particular cases, and sensitivity to the
cognitive situation of others are abundantly dem-
onstrated. The book of Job shows how far human
philosophy can go when facing the most difficult
questions of all.

Beyond Ancient Opinions

A reading of the book of Job forms the centerpiece
of the discussion of providence in *Guide of the Perplexed*, written in the twelfth century CE. For the
medieval Jewish philosopher, the book of Job is a
parable, and one "to which extraordinary notions
and things that are the mystery of the universe are at-
tached," making clear the highest of truths (III.22;
486).[6] Maimonides' reading of the book of Job offers the project of the whole *Guide* in miniature,
helping those followers of the Law unsettled by
questions raised by philosophical study to persevere
in faith and in philosophical inquiry.

The *Guide*, Maimonides explains at its start, is
written to explain "equivocal" language and parables. But the truths it explicates are not wrapped
in parables unnecessarily. They are disguised from
the ignorant multitude, but some are also the

sorts of insights whose *nature* it is to appear only in glimpses. "My purpose is that the truths be glimpsed and then again concealed, so as not to oppose that divine purpose . . . which has concealed from the vulgar . . . those truths specially requisite for His apprehension" (Introduction, 6–7). Determining what those esoteric truths are has occupied interpreters of Maimonides ever since.

If the *Guide* offers glimpses and then covers them up again, it is not only to safeguard teachings it is prohibited to spread, but also to characterize the nature of knowing itself. Knowledge of God is not like human ways of knowing. The only way for us to describe God is "by means of negations" (I.58; 134). For instance, when it is asserted of God "that He is powerful and knowing and willing," all that can be meant is "that He is neither powerless nor ignorant nor inattentive nor negligent" (I.58; 146). Yet the discussion of providence that culminates in Maimonides' parabolic reading of the book of Job seems to promise more.

The *Guide*'s introduction offers three parables about parables (11). In the first, parables are likened to the cords Solomon tied together to reach the pure water of truth at the bottom of a well. In the second, a parable is likened to a taper someone might light to find a pearl he has lost in the dark, and could never otherwise have found. Finally, a parable is like a golden apple in silver filigree— filigree whose tiny apertures make the gold visible to those who attend carefully. Parables can thus have a more than instrumental value. A taper is consumed as it illuminates, but a silver vessel is of value, too, and should be as beautiful as silver—though not as beautiful as gold. The "external meaning" of the "parables of the prophets" "contains wisdom that is useful in many respects, among which is the welfare of human societies . . . Their internal meaning, on the other hand, contains wisdom that is useful for beliefs concerned with the truth as it is" (Introduction; 12). Solomon accessed the well water of truth one bucket at a time with cords not one of which, on its own, could have sufficed.

In the first of many references to the positions laid out in Baba Bathra, Maimonides argues for the parabolic value of the book of Job with reference to the unnamed sage who said, "Job has not existed and was not created, but is a parable" (III.22, 486; cf. Baba Bathra, hereafter *BB*, 15a). As we saw earlier, he argues that the story's meaning is "equivocal" and Uz, while perhaps also the name of a place, is "the imperative of a verb meaning to reflect and meditate . . . It is as if [Scripture] said to you: Meditate and reflect on this parable" (III.22; 486–87).

The book of Job's parabolic nature is made clear also by the mythological beginning. God has no sons. The "sons of God" (1:6, 2:1) represent, rather, the forces of nature.

Satan, who comes to the divine court from the realm of accident, represents privation. Another sage from Baba Bathra is invoked: "Satan, the evil inclination, and the angel of death are one and the same" (III.22; 489; cf. *BB* 16a). Maimonides argues etymologically that the name *Satan* "derives from the notion of turning-away and going-away" (III.22; 489). The evil inclination, identified earlier in the *Guide* with imagination (II.12), "is produced in the individual at his birth" but "the *good inclination* is only found in man when his intellect is perfected" (III.22; 489–90).

It is crucial to appreciate, therefore, that when God commends his servant Job (1:8, 2:3) "knowledge is not attributed to Job" but only virtuous action (III.22; 487). Job's ignorant view, articulated once pressed, is that God treats the good and the evil equally "because of His contempt for the human species and abandonment of it" (III.23; 491, referring to 9:22–23 and 21:23–26). Maimonides cites Baba Bathra's condemnations of this view, but also its concession that "A man is not to be blamed for [what he does when] suffering" (III.23; 492; cf. *BB* 16b). The point is that Job *learns*. From knowledge based on authority he progresses to "certain knowledge":

> [H]e admitted that true happiness, which is the knowledge of the deity, is guaranteed to all who know Him and that a human being cannot be troubled in it by any of all the misfortunes in question. (III.23; 492–93)

This is the promise of the book of Job, and of the *Guide*.

Maimonides does not pass over the false claims of Job and his friends but dwells on them, indeed parses them. They may all sound the same on first reading, but if one seeks out the subtle differences one will see that Job and his friends represent the full range of philosophical reflection on providence. It may take a parabolic eye to see such clear and clearly distinct views here, but it makes sense that Job's three (or four) interlocutors should represent distinct views and that they should in some way be representative. Saadiah Gaon, the first great Jewish philosophical commentator on the book of Job, already identified Job's friends with Christian and Muslim critics of Israel. In an early modern manuscript they represent Catholic, Protestant, and Muslim views.[7] In Archibald MacLeish's play *J. B.*, they will represent the faiths of Christianity, psychoanalysis, and Marxism.

For Maimonides, Job's dispute with his friends is *structurally* congenial as well. The discussion of the book of Job follows his discussion of the "ancient opinions" on providence, just as the theophany follows the asseverations of Job and his friends. Maimonides finds that the

> opinion attributed to Job is in keeping with the opinion of Aristotle; the opinion of Eliphaz is in keeping with the opinion of our Law; the opinion of Bildad is in keeping with the doctrine of the Mu'tazila; the opinion of Zophar is in keeping with the doctrine of the Ash'ariyya. (III.23; 494)

It's hard to say which is more surprising—the linkage of Job with Aristotle or of the Law with Eliphaz. Aren't these the things being reconciled in the *Guide*? The breakthrough will come with Elihu, but before we turn to him, it's worth tarrying briefly with these "ancient opinions," for the philosophical problems they pose have not gone away.

In good Aristotelian fashion, Maimonides' discussion of providence began with a survey of received views. He found that philosophers had been "plung[ed]" or "impell[ed]" into erroneous opinions because of a common misunderstanding. Pushing them is "what appears at first sight to be a lack of order in the circumstances of the human individuals": the prospering of the wicked while the virtuous are afflicted (III.16; 461). The natural response, Maimonides observes, is to suppose fatalistically that things happen "by chance and in accordance with the way things were predestined; and that there is no one who orders, governs, or is concerned with anything" (III.17; 464). This fatalism is the first of the five views of providence Maimonides enumerates, all of them "ancient" (contemporary with the prophets) but still tracing the limits of philosophical thought.

Fatalism is identified with Epicurus. A second ancient opinion, in response, holds that providence watches over some things but not others—over species but not individuals. Maimonides describes this as the view of Aristotle, and commends it insofar as it "follow[s] what is manifest in the nature of that which exists" (III.17; 468), but it too leads to an abhorrent view, the opinion that "The Lord hath forsaken the earth [Ezek. 9·9]" (466). The third opinion, provoked by the second, insists that nothing ever happens by chance. Everything is the result of a divine will (466). This view, found among the Ash'ariyya (a school of Islamic thought subordinating reason to revelation), rightly rejects the idea of divine ignorance (468). It, too, has intolerable consequences, however, allowing no difference between the death of a human being and the fall of a leaf. Worse, there is no room for free will—and thus no purpose for the Law (467).

The fourth opinion, associated with the Mu'tazila (a rationalist school of Islamic thought), recoils from the contradictions of the third. Insisting on the perfect justice of God, it asserts that creations (even animals) are free, and that God acts wisely in rewarding and punishing them for their acts (III.17; 467). Yet this too leads to "incongruities and contradictions." When someone is born with an infirmity, one is obliged to believe that it is to his benefit. And if a great sage dies young, one must suppose that he will get his reward in the other world. Worse, God owes the same to animals (468). The Aristotelian, Ash'arite, and Mu'tazalite opinions are in error, yet Maimonides insists that their advocates should not "be blamed, for every one of them was impelled by strong necessity to say what he did." They are rather to be commended for their fidelity to the shape of experience and for their rejection of objection-able ideas of divine ignorance or impotence (III.17; 468). In their negations, they are not in error.

"The fifth opinion is our opinion, I mean the opinion of our Law" (III.17; 469). It asserts that humans (and animals) are free by divine volition, and that God responds to free acts with just punish-ment or reward, although "we are ignorant of the various modes of deserts" (III.17; 469). This sounds a lot like the fourth opinion, especially when Maimonides rejects the view (decisive for Saadiah Gaon) that one might suffer for others. But then he adds a view he identifies as his own:

> I do not believe that anything is hidden from him, may He be exalted, nor do I attribute to Him a lack of power. But I believe that providence is consequent upon the intellect and attached to it.... everyone with whom something of this overflow is united, will be reached by providence to the extent to which he is reached by the intellect. (III.17; 474)

In one of his most challenging arguments, Maimonides asserts that providence is "graded," watching more closely over more perfected intellects (III.18, 475). Moral virtue on its own is not enough to ensure the protection of providence.

All of the "ancient opinions" reappear in the exegesis of the book of Job that follows. The dialogue is a parabolic representation of the value of philosophical dispute. In their negations, if not in their affirmations, Job's and his friends' views had merit. But notice that the attributions do not quite square with the descriptions Maimonides has given of the ancient views. Job's view is really closer to that attributed to Epicurus. And "our Law," linked to Eliphaz, seems to be one of the views rejected by God. This being Maimonides, noticing the wrinkled surface of the text is the easy part. Discerning the esoteric truth beneath its filigree is another matter entirely.

Maimonides' own view appears in the speeches of Elihu—surprising to moderns, but an established element in medieval Jewish interpretation.[8] Most of what Elihu says is not new. If one attends to what has not been said before, however, one will discover "the one [opinion] that is intended." It is disguised as one would expect a truth available only in glimpses to be: as a parable within a parable. The idea Elihu adds "is that which he expresses parabolically when he speaks of the intercession of an angel" at 33:23 ("a mediator, one of a thousand, one who declares a person upright . . ."), supplemented by an account of "the how of prophecy" at 33:29–30 ("God indeed does all these things, twice, three times, with mortals, to bring back their souls from the Pit, so that they may see the light of life") (III.23; 495). The divine speeches demonstrate what Elihu alludes to, giving Job a "prophetic revelation." Maimonides lays out Elihu's view and the theophany in tandem, a striking demonstration of the way a perfected intellect can enjoy the perspective of providence.

But here the taper goes out. We have found the pearl, but cannot see it. As Elihu had anticipated, the "prophetic revelation" of the divine speeches does not go beyond the description of nature (III.23; 496). Job, too, achieves understanding by negation.

[O]ur intellects do not reach the point of apprehending how these natural things that exist in the world of generation and corruption are produced in time and of conceiving how the existence of the natural force within them has originated them. They are not things that resemble what we make. How then can we wish that His governance of, and providence for, them ... should resemble our governance of, and providence for, the things we do govern and provide for? (III.23; 496)

Nevertheless, something beyond negation has been achieved, for divine providence is sensed, and if "man knows this, every suffering will be borne lightly by him." Even "misfortunes will not add to his doubts regarding the deity," and every experience, whether it seems providential by our lights or not, will "add to his love" (ibid.).

How to understand all this is another question. The angels, including the angel of death = Satan = imagination, may be natural forces, or natural events. It may be that what allows the perfected individual to escape evil and misfortune is just psychological insight into the scientific nature of reality. Maimonides does not mention the restoration of Job's goods. His account ends with an injunction not to dwell on any details of the story besides those he's highlighted. The book's message is not to be found on the surface level of the story.

But what do we do with Maimonides' unpacking of the book of Job's teaching on providence? How do we avoid its becoming, again, an opinion? The study of nature, or natural philosophy, is evidently central to avoiding the errors of the ancient opinions on providence. But God can be known only with the aid of parable and equivocation, in a space cleared by negation of positive claims about divinity. For this the book of Job, precisely in its parabolic form, can be our guide. To hold on to an idea of providence that is like ours only in name, we must understand how what is manifest in existence impels us to philosophize. This is what the endless loop of ancient opinions of providence does. Each opinion is valuable as a way of avoiding an error to which we might legitimately be driven, though it goes too far. Speculation may enable us to understand and participate in providence, but the temptation to affirmation must be checked. The ancient opinions are like cords we can tie together to get a taste of the pure water of a providence beyond our ken, but not beyond our participation.

Providence and Pedagogy

For Maimonides, the philosophical opinions of Job and his friends cancel each other out, making way for an apprehension of divine providence. The divine speeches present a God beyond all human categories, and take no cognizance of human experience or questions. For Christian theologian Thomas Aquinas, the book of Job is a philosophical discussion, too. It is analogous to the structured debates at the heart of the curriculum of the University of Paris. And although God ultimately decides the debate, in Aquinas' interpretation it is his servant Job who is the main teacher, for Job is a "friend of God" (89; on Job 1:21).[9] Like earlier commentators who understood the book of Job as a debate, Aquinas brings a real sensitivity to the text's drama and nuance, and even manages to present the exchanges of Job and his friends as addressing each other, not talking past each other. Only one dispute escapes his notice: that of Job with God.

Aquinas wrote commentaries on many books of the Bible, as well as on works of Aristotle, Boethius, and others. For Job he wrote only a "literal exposition." Gregory the Great had already taken care of the spiritual meanings of the text, Aquinas explained. In fact Aquinas contributed decisively to a renewed emphasis on the literal sense

of scripture. While his conception of the literal includes many things earlier interpreters understood
as allegorical—metaphors, even prophecies—in
the case of Job the literal meaning was important
for another reason. It is preeminently a book about
philosophical argumentation, and arguments require clear, stable terms.

The book of Job is a debate about providence.
Aquinas believed it had been written right after
the books of the Law, as evil is the first challenge
to "reverence for or fear of God" (68). In his most
influential work, the *Summa Theologica*, Aquinas
introduces evil as the first objection to arguments
for the existence of God.[10] The Job exposition was
written while Aquinas was writing the discussion
of providence in *Summa Contra Gentiles*, another
major work. In all his discussions of evil, Aquinas
follows the Neoplatonic and Augustinian tradition
which understands evil as privation. (Maimonides
also shared this view.) Properly understood, evil is
not a substance, but parasitic deprivation or distor-
tion of created substances all of which are, in their
essence, good. Aquinas recalls the broader framing
of the problem of evil in *The Consolation of Philosophy*: "Boethius introduces a certain philosopher
who asks: 'If God exists, whence comes evil?' But it
could be argued to the contrary: 'If evil exists, God
exists.'"[11] The substances on which evil parasitically

depends are by nature good and come from God. The understanding of evil as privation is not the denial of a difference between good and evil. It rejects metaphysical dualism but also steers clear of the Stoic view that we should ultimately be indifferent to all things of this world. Evil involves real harm and loss.

In the book of Job, Aquinas finds an enactment of the argument that "if evil exists, God exists." According to Aquinas, the book's "whole intention . . . turns on showing through plausible arguments that human affairs are ruled by providence" (68). We're in the realm of what philosophers of religion today call the "evidential problem of evil"—whether the nature of our experience doesn't in fact tell against the existence of an omipotent and just God. The toughest case is not the prosperity of the wicked, which could be explained in terms of divine mercy toward them,

> But that just men should be afflicted without cause seems to undermine totally the foundation of providence. Therefore, there are proposed for the intended discussion as a kind of theme the many grave afflictions of a certain man, perfect in every virtue, named Job. (68)

The debaters are Job and his friends, and Job exemplifies the right understanding of evil from the start.

Aquinas commends Job for the quality of his lament, for instance. To say that "the Lord gave, and the Lord has taken away" is not to say that the things given and taken are indifferent:

> [I]t is the mark of friends to want and to reject the same things. Hence, if it proceeds from divine good pleasure that someone be despoiled of his temporal goods, if he loves God he ought to conform his own will to the divine will, so that considering this he should not be engrossed by sadness. (89; on Job 1:21)

In his acts of mourning, Job shows an appropriate grief at the destruction of true goods: "not to be pained over dead loved-ones seems to be the mark of a hard and insensitive heart." Yet he showed "such moderate sadness that it was subject to reason" (87–88; on Job 1:21). Because the goods of life are true goods, but not the only or highest goods, Aquinas also has less difficulty than many interpreters with the ultimate restoration of Job's fortunes. Job did not seek it but God restored his prosperity, as promised in the gospel of Matthew (6:33): "Strive first for the kingdom of God and his righteousness, and all these things will be given to you as well" (472; on Job 42:10).

In accordance with his understanding of the goods of life as true goods, Aquinas knows that pain is real and has real effects. For Gregory pain served to wrench us from sinful attachment to the world, and was so necessary for human discernment that the real question was why God did not afflict all his favored. Aquinas sees a medicinal value in pain as well, but his fundamental view is that pain does not free the spirit but oppresses it: "By being weighed down, the soul is not free to take an interest in things outside itself; it shrinks into itself and contracts."[12] Job's shocking wish never to have been born, once affliction hits, is not only understandable but in its way reasonable: "although being and living, considered in itself, is desirable, yet being and living in misery in a situation of this kind is to be renounced" (110; on Job 3:1).

We have seen already in Baba Bathra the view that some of Job's strongest statements were uttered under the duress of grief and pain. We should understand that he was beside himself as he said them; in a real sense they were not his words at all. It was the pain speaking. Aquinas sets many of the passages modern readers think most truly Job's aside in this way. What we should learn from them is that even a friend of God can be pushed to his limits by pain and loss—but also that a figure like Job is able, even in these awful circumstances, to avoid blasphemy. The key for Aquinas' reading is God's judgment that Job spoke rightly in Chapter

42. Although Job evidently had prideful thoughts for which he repented, he never sinned with his lips. Throughout the philosophical exchanges with his friends, Job is in a state of pain great enough to push even the holy to despair. If he sometimes forgets himself, we should be understanding, and not credit those words to him.

The word Aquinas uses for the "disputation" is *quaestio*, the standard format for university debates. In a disputation a question is posed, and before an argument is given for what will be the proffered right answer, the strongest objections to this view are critically analyzed. This critique does not make reference to the as-yet-unmade argument for the correct view, but takes the objections apart in their own terms. No view is entirely mistaken, so there is something to be learned from engaging each one seriously. After the best objections have been heard (there can be dozens), the correct answer to the question is presented. It is introduced by an appeal to authority, usually biblical or patristic, although Aristotle ("the Philosopher") is invoked too. The appeal to authority seems a mere formality in many cases. The *quaestio* is won or lost on the basis of argumentation, not authority. But in the most important cases, an inspired source reveals a truth human beings could not discover or validate on their own. The approved view is then applied to all issues raised by the objections.

Approaching the book of Job as a disputation makes more sense of it than one might at first think. The exchanges with the friends are structured in three cycles with responses. At the end, the matter is "decided" by the same one who posed it—God. While in a sense the appearance of God is a formality—Aquinas' Job has already laid out the correct view—God does make an indispensable contribution. No human being can *know* God's will. Our knowledge of God, his nature and will, can only be "analogical": in ways only God comprehends, words used of God and created beings have different but related meanings.[13] Already in his reference to the "foundation of the earth" (38:4), however, God answers the providence question.

The point is not to know providence—we cannot—but to trust in it. Job is able to do so because he knows something his friends do not: that this life is not all there is. This awareness isn't just pie in the sky but "increases the intelligibility of the world."[14] Job's friends, ignorant of it, are driven to perjure themselves, to show an ungodly favoritism for God. Secure in his prophetic knowledge of the afterlife, Job is able to acknowledge that this world does not, in fact, make sense at all:

After Job has shown through cogent arguments that the consolation of Eliphaz, who was promising earthly prosperity, was inconsistent, he now shows by a reduction to absurdities that, if he were to rely on that consolation which had been given him by Eliphaz based on the hope of earthly prosperity, since that hope is frivolous, . . . he would still have to remain in sadness, to utter words of sorrow, and to despair completely. (150; on Job 7:11)

What the friends hear as Job's blasphemy is actually an unvarnished account of reality.

Job wants his friends to acknowledge that, based on their own this-worldly retributionist assumptions, there really is no compelling evidence of providence in our experience—a crucial step toward seeing the insufficiency of this world. Yet news of an afterlife is not easy for those unaware of it to grasp or even conceive. Aquinas' Job articulates it in stages, slowly, starting in chapter 7, a bit more clearly at 14:5, and then explicitly in 19:25. But Job's friends still cannot hear him. Besides, Job is not making the crass argument that in the afterlife all scores are settled, a kind of posthumous vindication of retributionist logic. Divine justice, too, is only analogically like our own. In fact "man's present life does not have in it [eternity] the ultimate end but is compared to it as motion is compared to rest and the road to the destination" (145; on Job 7).

When God decides the debate he condemns the friends for speaking wrongly of him, something Aquinas has already done: "divine goodness and justice do not need a lie for their defense, since truth can be defended without a lie" (215; on Job 13:7–8). Elihu comes in for special sanction for having presumed to decide the debate. But Job is reproved, too—for being a bad teacher. Through his efforts to show his friends the error of their ways, "scandal was produced" in their hearts (415; on Job 38:1–2).

Aquinas shares with many modern interpreters the view that Job does not, at least at first, articulate a position of his own, but rather is provoked to speak by the claims of his friends. He works within the universe of their assumptions to refute and transcend them, with a bitter sarcasm that further scandalized them. At other times (and some of the same times) he nearly loses himself in pain. (We are perhaps too fortunate to know how such pain addles the mind; for reasons that may have more to do with the existential situation of our secular age discussed in chapter 5, we may too quickly accept the idea of pain as a teacher.) It can be a comfort to see a great man like Job, a friend of God no less, showing both the fragility of human self-possession and the possibility that one might, in the midst of the greatest torments, not lose oneself entirely.

To a contemporary reader, however, Aquinas' sensitivity and ingenuity also conveniently shield him from seeing that Job may actually have come close to rebellion. Even if Job knew all that Aquinas supposes him to have known of providence and of pedagogy, should not a consideration of the full extent of unjust suffering in God's creation have caused scandal in *him*? So attentive to the ways we hear and respond to each other, Aquinas wasn't able to hear that most, perhaps all, of Job's speeches were addressed not to his friends but to God.

Breaking Point

What we today take to be Job's true voice finally comes through when the reformer John Calvin comes to listen to Job, in the course of a series of sermons delivered during the period 1554–55. Job sounds to Calvin like a rebel. He is a better man than we can ever be, but his protest should not be an example to us. We may "have no intent to blaspheme God" but duress inclines us to "be overhardy in our talk, like as when Job desired to have all his sayings registered and engraved for an everlasting remembrance, and printed in stone or lead, to the

intent it might never be blotted out [19:23–24]."[15]
Calvin commends David's example over Job's: "we
must learn to keep our mouth shut when God afflicts us" (ibid.). And yet the attention demanded
by 159 sermons, each devoted to only a few lines of
the biblical text, took Calvin closer to seeing what
Job saw: "the instability of Providence and the
darker side of God's nature."[16]

The book of Job plays an important role in Calvin's theological masterpiece, the *Institutes of the
Christian Religion*. God's granting Satan permission to act confirmed that God alone is in charge,
something Job understood in regarding his afflictions as coming from God (1.17.7 and 8; 2.4.2). Job's
concession that all human beings are impure—
"Who can bring a clean thing out of an unclean?
No one can" (14:4)—confirmed original sin (2.1.5).
Job's confidence in a redeemer is cited too, but carefully, as Calvin did not believe in prophetic knowledge. Job could not have *known* of a redeemer, but
he could know that redemption was to be wished
(2.10.19 and 3.25.4). The Hymn to Wisdom (Chapter 28) confirmed that God's wisdom is hidden
from us (1.17.2).

More important for Calvin's argument, the book
of Job shows that God is so high above his creation
that even the canons of justice he sets out for us are

not ultimate. Beyond them God has a higher justice, before which none can stand.

> All must immediately perish, as Job declares,
> "Shall mortal man be more just than God? shall
> a man be more pure than his Maker? Behold,
> he put no trust in his servants; and his angels he
> charged with folly: How much less in them that
> dwell in houses of clay, whose foundation is in
> the dust, which are crushed before the moth?
> They are destroyed from morning to evening,"
> (Job 4:17–20). Again, "Behold, he putteth
> no trust in his saints; yea, the heavens are not
> clean in his sight. How much more abominable
> and filthy is man, which drinketh iniquity like
> water?" (Job 15:15, 16) (3.12.1)[17]

Disclosed here is the most difficult and important teaching concerning God and his providence: God's is a double justice, a double providence. The book of Job presents this in several ways, from the prologue to the divine speeches, and in the inspired speeches of human beings as well.

The observant reader might have noticed that the passages just cited—Job 4:17–20 and 15:15–16—are words not of Job but of Eliphaz. In the course of his sermons, Calvin also sometimes treats these words as Job's. There is in fact a long history of attributing Eliphaz' dream to Job, but Calvin has no need of this hypothesis. All of the book of Job is inspired. Many of its most important teachings come not from Job but from his friends, and even more from Elihu. As we have seen, this is part of what makes reading the book of Job such a delicate task for orthodox thinkers.

Calvin's concern is not just which teachings are true but how to live with these truths. Here he, like Aquinas before him, attends to the nature of the exchanges between Job and his friends. The key to the text, and its most important practical teaching, is that "in all this disputation, Job maintains a good case, and contrariwise his adversaries maintain an evil case." Job was right to insist that suffering did not indicate sin: God has his "secret judgments" which men cannot know. Job's case, however, is "ill handled." He "ranges ... out of his bounds, and uses such excessive and outrageous talk, that in many points he seems a desperate person." Indeed, "it seems that he would even resist God."[18]

Job's friends, meanwhile, "undertake the evil case" but with

> goodly and holy sentences, and there is nothing
> in their whole talk which would not entice us
> to receive it as if the holy Ghost himself had ut-
> tered it. For it is plain truth: they be the grounds
> of religion: they treat of God's providence: they
> treat of his justice: they treat of men's sins ...

doctrine which we must receive without gain-saying: and yet the drift of it is evil.[19]

The friends' mechanical application of general biblical truth to the particular case of Job is misguided. They are unaware of God's double justice. Elihu will be the one to explain the many reasons for which God might afflict those he loves. The real question raised by both Job and his friends is the same: how to understand divine providence in particular cases. Job shows how not to understand one's own suffering. The friends show how not to respond to another's suffering.

Job's mistake, based in his understanding of God's higher justice and secret judgments, was to think himself abandoned, and to forget that in the Bible God "accommodates" himself to his creations.[20] God goes so far as to "stammer and lisp with us when he sees it meet and convenient for us."[21] While none can stand in the face of God's power and wisdom, God graciously grants humans not to judge them by his hidden judgments but only by those he has shared with them. Job forgets the better part of the good news, seeing God only as the tyrant he is entitled to be—but, given his love, never in fact will be.[22]

[W]e must not enclose God's mighty power within our imagination and understanding. Like as God's goodness is endless and a bottomless pit: so also are his wisdom and righteousness, and the same is to be said of his power.... And seeing that God's mighty power is not to be measured nor to be enclosed and made subject to worldly and natural means: our belief also must stretch out both high and low, and become infinite.[23]

As our words inevitably are finite in meaning, we do best to "keep our mouth shut" when, like Job, we encounter affliction. It is a fearful thing when God pleases to "hide himself"—"enough to overwhelm the whole world"[24]—but we should trust that God has his reasons. As Calvin preached on Job, the Protestants in Paris were starting to suffer the persecution that would end in the Saint Bartholomew's Day massacre. They must not understand their affliction as abandonment by God.

What made the drift of the friends' case evil was that they pushed Job toward despair. Even if everything they said was true at the general level, the appropriate response to a fellow who is suffering is to rescue him from despair, not to push him toward it. In the sermons on the book of Job, Calvin has the opportunity to discuss every word and every passage both for its theological truth and for its applicability to life. The lesson throughout is that God is greater and more mysterious than the Law.

"[W]hen the Scripture shows us who or what we be: it is to make us utterly nothing."²⁵ But God also judges his human subjects mercifully, and so should we. The humbling awareness of being worthless before God should create solidarity between mortals, not judgment.

The book of Job, then, is a resource not only of important theological teachings like that of God's double justice. It is a resource for understanding the difficulty of maintaining faith in a providence that necessarily exceeds our comprehension in our actual lives. Both Job and his friends have pieces of the full story but misapply them in the particular case. Job, knowing himself no worse a sinner than others, thinks himself abandoned by a tyrannical and capricious God. The friends, knowing God's commitment to the Law, presume to know that God has judged Job. True faith expresses itself not as they do but as humility and silence in the sufferer, solicitude and comfort in others:

> [W]hen we see a poor offender whom God has put to execution, we must be touched in our-selves, and that for two causes. The one is that if every of us look into himself, we shall find that God ought to punish us as roughly or roughlier, if it pleased him to visit us according to our des-erts.... Again, ... let us consider not only that

he was created after the image of God: but also that he is our neighbor and in manner all one with us.[26]

The balance is achieved most nearly by the one character God does not reprove. Elihu sees that Job is not being punished but that he errs in thinking himself just before God. Calvin sees in Elihu "proof that from ancient times some good 'seed of religion' survived in the midst of darkness."[27] In fact, Calvin uses the exposition of Elihu's speeches to provide a compendium of his own theology.

And yet, abiding with Job through the many moments of his anguish can be a terrifying experience; "the sovereignty of Job's God scared even Calvin."[28] Perhaps God not only *could* be a tyrant but is. Arguably this is Job's discomfiting discovery as he moves from a faith in God's secret judgments to a growing awareness of a pattern of human misfortune that suggests that God's nature is arbitrary judgment, not love. "We see the wicked reign," Calvin preached, " . . . and to our seeming God is all that while asleep in heaven: and when he remedies not things at the first dash, we think he doth not his duty."[29] The problem is so great that only God can solve it, even if this means that God must protect Job from God himself. The awareness of God's secret judgment would lead even the saints to despair

Job in Disputation   111 or madness, if God did not sustain them with hope. Even as Job felt abandoned, the very fact that he was able to persist in demanding understanding is in truth a sign of divine succor.

The book of Job helps the Calvin of the *Institutes* lay out an understanding of the transcendence of a God whose justice goes beyond what we can grasp. The sermons' close attention to the claims of each of the characters in the book of Job shows another side of Calvin's understanding of the human condition. God both endorses and exceeds our categories of justice, and can subject his human creations to experiences that push them toward the abyss of thinking him a tyrant in order to help them understand this. When this happens to our fellows, however, we are called not to judge but to support each other. Every word of the book of Job, including the words of Eliphaz, Bildad, and Zophar, contains precious truth. But the book of Job also contains a warning about the difficulty of applying biblical truth in practice, a difficulty grounded not only in God's hidden purposes but in the frightening otherness Calvin discovered during his sojourn with Job.

Calvin's efforts to assert a double justice for God lead him to the edge of paradox, and his character Job is driven to the edge of rebellion and despair. Sociologist of religion Max Weber saw in Calvin the nadir of monotheistic thinking on the problem of evil—the inevitable failure of the religious effort to make of this "ethically irrational" world a "meaningful cosmos." Only three

> systems of ideas on the whole . . . gave rationally satisfactory answers to the questioning for the basis of the incongruity between destiny and merit: the Indian doctrine of [k]arma, Zoroastrian dualism, and the predestination decree of the [Calvinist] *deus absconditus*.[30]

But rationality has reached a breaking point here. Calvinism's rejection of the possibility of a "rational solution" to the problem of evil "conceals the greatest tension between the world and god, between the actually existent and the ideal."[31] This tension produced an unprecedented inner isolation as individuals sought to affirm a general providential design they could not discern in particular cases—including their own status as elect or reprobate. Weber saw Calvinist "salvation anxiety" undermine traditional religious meanings and practices and lead ineluctably to the "disenchantment" of the modern world. As channeled especially by the book of Job, the ancient problem of evil defeated religious efforts to make the world a home.

No medieval or early modern thinker believed that the world could make sense in its own terms, however—or should. Not all would agree with

Martin Luther's view that "God so orders this corporeal world in its external affairs that if you respect and follow the judgment of human reason, you are bound to say either that there is no God or that God is unjust."[32] Many, however, thought the frank acknowledgment of the insufficiency of unaided human reason to be the first step toward wisdom— the wisdom that, as Chapter 28 of the book of Job made clear, God alone knows and human beings search for in vain.

As we have followed the interpretations of the book of Job in Maimonides, Aquinas, and Calvin, we have noticed something else, too. An honest confrontation with the problem of providence puts us in our place, which is far from God (though he approaches us) but near to our fellows. Speculation about providence is a social act, and should be done in an ethical way. For Maimonides, the ancient opinions correct each other, clearing a space for an equivocal understanding of providence to appear, if only in glimpses. Aquinas argued that we should learn to have compassion for those whose suffering pushes them to the edge of despair and madness, and also that we have a responsibility to help each other, not to cause scandal in each other. And in Calvin, finally, who seems closest to hearing the voice we take now to have been Job's all along, we find a warning against driving others, even those who are probably being justly punished, into despair. Truths about providence can be misused.

It may seem that the movement from Maimonides' and Aquinas' medieval to Calvin's early modern understanding is one in which Job's protests slowly come to be heard. We might link this to a movement from allegorical and parabolical readings to the more literal readings of Calvin's quest for the "plain sense" of scripture. But we have also moved from a manual for philosophers to a commentary for theologians and finally to a series of sermons for a community. Proximity to the lived religion of actual sufferers surely made Job's voice harder to muzzle. Yet Job's anguished and despairing voice did not need rediscovering. As we will see in the next chapter, it had long been a part of liturgical and artistic life. Epicurus' old questions would not come into their own as the "problem of evil" until the modern period we explore in chapter 4.

Job Enacted

CHAPTER 3

It is sometimes claimed that only the modern age has had the courage to hear Job's voice, while pre-modern interpreters either tuned out his inspired rants and pleas, or construed them as expressions of weakness, vice, or pain-induced madness. We have seen a fair amount of such reframing, although we have found that most of it attends closely to Job's words and in fact validates Job's discovery that this world doesn't make moral sense. In this chapter we will see that Job's voice was one of the best known of biblical voices. If in philosophical readings Job's questions are somehow resolved, the settings in which Job's voice rang out in various kinds of enactment kept his questions ever alive.

In this chapter we seek an understanding of how the book of Job was encountered in the lives of ordinary people, not just philosophers and theologians. Job's anguish, and the danger implicit in his story

116

for faith in a just God, may have been more fully explored in ritual and performative contexts than in the interpretive glosses that have been our objects so far. After a survey of Job's place in liturgies and lectionaries ancient and modern, we will explore the powerful place Job has in rituals around death, and see the effects of his pained words rippling out into private devotional and public theatrical performances. We close with the story of Griselda, a literary female Job, whose experiences in a sequence of retellings show that, whatever religious authorities were telling them, lay people knew of the rebellious potential of Job's story.

Liturgies

The subjects of this chapter are taken from Christian tradition. Job does not have a prominent place in Jewish liturgy, perhaps because of his perceived significance as a gentile.[1] What was understood as Job's prophetic awareness of the coming of Christ and of the resurrection led the book of Job to be read from early on in the Easter season. In fourth-century Milan, the book of Job was read on the Wednesday of Holy Week. In other churches, selected chapters (19, 24, 26, 28, 30, 32) were read on Fridays in Lent. The choice of readings and the

timing of their inclusion make the connection between the sufferings of Job and Christ clear.[2]

Job was also venerated as a saint. From at least
the fourth century, pilgrims sought out his tomb.
(Several places still claim to house it, one of which
offers petrified worms as relics.) His feast day fell
on May 6 in the Western, and May 10 in the Eastern
Christian calendar.[3] The specialties Saint Job devel-
oped over the centuries—from leprosy to worms,
musicians, hen-pecked husbands, and eventually
syphilis—are anchored more in the legend of Job
than in the biblical book. Most of the important
artworks representing Job were commissioned for
churches or chapels dedicated to Saint Job.

Entry to the fourteenth-century church of San
Giobbe in Venice (a city that had a tradition of
venerating Old Testament figures as saints[4]) is still
made through a portal by Pietro Lombardo showing Saints Job and Francis on bended knee. Its
magnificent altarpiece by Giovanni Bellini, whose
juxtaposition of Saint Job with Saint Sebastian (re-
capitulated in his "Sacred Allegory") has led some
to conclude that Job was a patron saint for sexual
minorities,[5] now resides in the Accademia museum.[6] In plague-prone Flanders, a thousand-year-
old veneration of Job continues into our own time.
The church of Sint-Job in Schoonbroek, Belgium
only in 1991 stopped its procession around town

of the statue of the worm-infested Job which tops its splendid sixteenth-century carved altar. Sint-Job boasts a library of litanies to Saint Job from the seventeenth through the nineteenth centuries.

Our concern, however, is with the book of Job, regular reading of which became common in monastic communities in the West, converging eventually on August and September.[7] Each reading was followed by a catechized nugget of Job 2:10 and 1:21:

> RESPONSE: If we have received good things
> at the hand of God, why should we not
> receive evil? The Lord gave, and the Lord
> hath taken away: as it hath pleased the
> Lord so is it done: blessed be the name of
> the Lord.
> VERSICLE: Naked came I out of my mother's
> womb, and naked shall I return thither.[8]

In many breviaries, the reading of Job is followed immediately by a reading of the book of Tobit, which likens its long-suffering protagonist's patience to that of "holy Job" (2:12, 15). Chapters 1, 3, 9, 19, 38, and 42 of the book of Job were read in daily mass,[9] but the book of Job makes only two appearances on a Sunday: 7:1–7 and 38:1–11, chosen to complement gospel readings about healing and the calming of the sea, respectively. Job 14:1–14 is part of the Holy Saturday liturgy. The whole sweep of the book of Job was never encountered, however.

A somewhat better situation obtains in those Christian congregations today that avail themselves of an option in the Revised Common Lectionary decoupling Old Testament readings from the gospel; over a three-year cycle, all the books of the Old Testament are excerpted including Job.[10]

Job 1:1; 2:1–10
Job 23:1–9, 16–17
Job 38:1–7 [34–41]
Job 42:1–6, 10–17

The selections powerfully capture the arc of Job's story and the bitterness of his complaint. His story is made more universal by omitting mention of his great wealth, focusing instead on his individual affliction. (The death of his children is left out, too, though not the birth of new children at the story's end.) This selection also exemplifies current Christian and interfaith readings of the Old Testament as historical rather than typological. It omits the prophetic passages in Chapter 19 central to premodern Christian interpretations of the Book of Job.[11]

Job 19:23–27 has a life of its own as one of the readings available for funerals,[12] starting from Job's plea that his friends have pity on him and his wish

that his words might be written in a book, and cul-
minating in perhaps the most famous words in the
whole book of Job:

For I know that my Redeemer lives,
    and that at the last he will stand upon the
    earth;
and after my skin has been thus destroyed,
    then in my flesh I shall see God,
whom I shall see on my side,
    and my eyes shall behold, and not another.
    (Job 25–27a)

(We have seen that "Redeemer" is only one way to
translate *go'el*, but that is as nothing compared to
the obscurity of the next two verses.) The use of
these passages in funerals goes back to the ancient
memorial service known as the Office of the Dead.
Job's voice, in all its confusion and hopelessness,
was heard and performed with greater regularity
than perhaps any other voice besides those of Jesus,
David, and Mary. In these settings his was the voice
of everyman. Job showed how death and loss must
be faced.

It surprises many to learn that the anguished
Job should have been given voice at all. Ages of
faith are stereotyped as involving a collective refusal to acknowledge intellectual problems or even
doubts. We have seen these judgments in the ease

with which it's been assumed that premodern Jews and Christians simply ignored or shouted down the "impatient Job" of the dialogues. As we've seen, the story is more complicated. Job's words of complaint and protest were rarely taken at face value, it is true, but they were nevertheless heard, and contributed to a deeper understanding of patience. All of the book of Job, not just the pious frame story, came to define this virtue.

The passages we have been told premoderns refused to face were in fact not ignored but factored in to what patience means. Job's explosions of grief show what even the most holy are driven to by pain, loss, and the sense of divine abandonment. Since he was a moral paragon, however, commended by God for speaking rightly, Job's words show us what response to unmerited affliction is permissible and even appropriate. Job offers the licensed way to grieve. Submission was one part of it. Rage at misfortune and even at God was another.

Job was early made a central voice of the Christian burial liturgy. The Matins of the Burial of the Dead, probably established well before the seventh century (some evidence points to the second century), do not tell Job's story; the frame story is gone. Rather we hear Job's words—and not the words exchanged with his friends, but those addressed to God. These include his most strident speeches.

They are interwoven with similar sentiments from the Psalms attributed to David. (The Psalter is the spine of all the Offices, but these particular psalms are chosen to complement what Job says.) Where philosophical interpretations ignored or explained away Job's passionate emotions, here these emotions are front and center.[13]

Psalm 5, Psalm 6, Psalm 7

Job 7: 16–21

Spare me, for my days are nothing. . . .

Job 10: 1–7

My soul is weary of my life, . . . I will speak in the bitterness of my soul. . . .

Job 10: 8–12

Thy hands have made me, . . . do st thou thus cast me down headlong on a sudden? . . .

Psalm 22, Psalm 24, Psalm 27

Job 13: 23–28

How many are my iniquities and sins? make me know my crimes and offences . . .

Job 14: 1–6

Man born of a woman, living for a short time, is filled with many miseries. . . .

Job 14: 13–16

Who will grant me this, that thou mayst protect me in hell, and hide me till thy wrath pass, . . .

Psalm 39, Psalm 40, Psalm 41

Job 17: 1–3, 11–15

My spirit shall be wasted, my days shall be short-
ened, and only the grave remaineth for me. . . .

Job 19: 20–27

The flesh being consumed. My bone hath
cleaved to my skin, and nothing but lips are
left about my teeth. . . .

Job 10: 18–22

Why didst thou bring me forth out of the
womb: . . .

These are Job's darkest and most powerful words.
Between the readings reassuring responses, also
taken from the book of Job, are spoken or sung by
the congregation, at their heart a version of Job 25.
Congregants pledge, "I believe that my redeemer
lives . . .": "believe," not "know."

The interplay between Job's and David's words
and those of the congregation performs a kind of
community theater. Job speaks for the deceased.
When he comes to 19:25, and says "I *know* that my
redeemer lives" (italics added), it suggests that the
faith the believer takes with her into death will be
vindicated. But Job's voice, especially as echoed
and amplified by David's, is also the voice of every
mortal soul facing death. The theatrical quality of
this event suggests that we may need each other

to keep ourselves from despair. Conspicuously absent from the proceedings, however, are Job's friends with all their theologizing. The liturgical community, allowing Job to speak for himself, offers truer comfort.

The sequence of readings from the book of Job is chronological, suggesting an unfolding of awareness. But there is a dramatic reversal at the end. The first eight readings build to Job's confidence that he will one day see his redeemer in a resurrected body. The Office does not rest in this certainty; it ends back in the sense of dread and abandonment of Chapter 10. The Office of the Dead does not narrate a secure movement from darkness to light, from doubt to confidence. Job ends back in terror, and fear of a death without resurrection:

Why didst thou bring me forth out of the womb? O that I had been consumed, that eye might not see me!

I should have been as if I had not been, carried from the womb to the grave.

Shall not the fewness of my days be ended shortly? Suffer me, therefore, that I may lament my sorrow a little.

Before I go, and return no more: to a land that is dark and covered with the mist of death.

A land of misery and darkness, where the
shadow of death, and no order, but everlasting
horrow [sic] dwelleth. (10:18–22)

Scholars are not sure how these dark words ended
up here. They may have been added when the *Dies
Irae* emerged in the thirteenth century: having
broken through to awareness of resurrection, one
was confronted with a new terror, the terror of the
day of wrath.[14] Whatever the reason, Job's voice in
the burial office—the mandated voice of all facing
death—arrived at confidence only to fall back again
into despair. This makes profound psychological
sense. In place of sure knowledge it offers a community of struggling hope and solidarity.

The story of Job is as much one of breaking
through the blandishments of false comfort as of
arriving at a truer, more secure view. We can see the
looping back to Chapter 10 as awareness of the fragility of confidence. Faith in redemption is as difficult to achieve and maintain as lived patience or
confidence in providence. None of the theological
virtues is straightforward. They need to be understood as truncated and repeating narratives, not
once-for-all logical demonstrations or pledges of
faith, and they require constant sustenance. The
journey from despair to confidence, from grief to
hope, is traversed more than once. We struggle and

fail, again and again. We think we're in the clear, but the ground gives way again beneath our feet.

In ritual community we can support the fragile hope that individual human despair matters to an inscrutable creator. We should not be surprised at this roller-coaster-like structure. Theorists have long argued that the efficacy of ritual comes from the possibility of performing together ideas that cannot be thought together. Phenomenological accounts of the old Catholic mass show that it, too, enacts not a single movement but a repeated approaching and reapproaching of divine presence, often finding oneself back at square one.[15]

Participating in Job's despair and hope may be particularly valuable in the vertiginous experience of facing one's death. Job is a liminal figure, at the boundary of the covenant. Job's own ritual life is merely gestured at. It seems to have been an implicit individual arrangement with God, and part of his agony comes out of the apparent destruction of the relationship he thought he had with the divine. God, whom he had earlier had good reason to suppose a friend, now has singled him out as an enemy. Job speaks for all who feel the apparatus of their lives collapse about them. David is usually a comfort because believers are thought to stand in a relation to God more like David's than Job's—there *is* a liturgical tradition, a law, a covenant. David has

much to atone for, as we do, but has found absolution. In the moment of hopelessness and rage at suffering we cannot understand, however, we are like
Job. Nothing that has made sense in the past makes
sense any longer, and we may wish that none of it
had ever happened.

The Office of the Dead is strong medicine, treat-
ing anguish with anguish. It acknowledges that a
sense of abandonment is part of the relationship
with a transcendent God, and that the apparent injustice of God's mysterious ways may make it seem
better never to have been born. It does more than
acknowledge these reactions. It authorizes them.
The impassioned passages from the Book of Job
kept alive in the Office of the Dead offer language
for our own grief and confusion and despair, which
it lets us express at once in the bitterness of our soul
and in blessed community.

The dramatic therapeutic power of Job's dark-
est, most desperate words has been dropped from
Catholic liturgy and life, however. Already excluded
from the liturgy, Vatican II all but excised Job from
the Matins of the Office of the Dead as well.[16] The
Job readings have been replaced by readings from
Paul's Epistle to the Corinthians. The only trace of
Job that remains is 19:25–27a in one of the responses.
What was traditionally understood to be the most
difficult thing to achieve, in its way the flickering

climax of the rite, is reduced to a familiar cliché. Has faith become so much easier? Or have the liturgists lost their nerve, concerned that Job's importunate words—available now in the vernacular—would raise questions too strong for faith?

Personal Jobs

In the medieval world, the Office of the Dead was not heard only in monastic communities. It was frequently included in the Books of Hours that were like lectionaries for lay people, and often appeared in vernacular translation (see figure 7). Reciting the Office of the Dead daily was recommended for the pious lay person (often a woman), as it was for clergy. Books of Hours are now known best for their opulent illustrations. Even those with relatively few and simple illustrations often included an image of Job on his ash or dung heap opposite the Office of the Dead. If in liturgies mourners experienced Job's voice circulating around the community of the living and the dead, in private performance his words became the reader's. Job and his story came to stand alone in our imaginations less because of the emergence of Bibles without *glossae* than because his words had already become our words in this most private of settings.

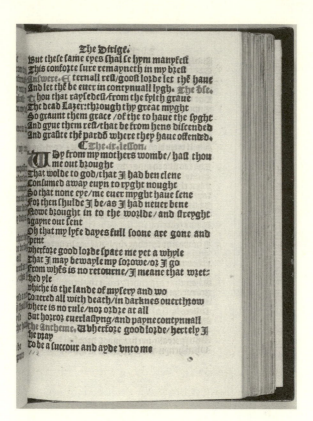

Figure 7. Speeches of Job formed the core of the Office of the Dead, an ancient Christian practice that was spread from monasteries to pious lay people in Books of Hours. In this English *Prymer* after the Sarum Rite, printed in France in 1538, Job's anguished words in Chapter 10 are rendered in rhyme. PML 19585. *Here after foloweth the prymer in Englysshe sette out alonge : after the use of Sarum.*, fol. 112r. Rowen: By Nycholas le Roux for Franchoys Regnault, 1538. © The Pierpont Morgan Library, New York. PML 19585. Photo by The Pierpont Morgan Library, New York.

The nine readings from Job in the Matins of the Office of the Dead were also available on their own. In early fifteenth-century England they were set as a long devotional/contritional poem known as "Pety Job." Operating outside the context of the Office of the Dead, without responses and versicles and without the leveling effect of the Psalms, "Pety Job" identified the reader completely with Job. The last line of each of its fifty-seven stanzas is *Parce michi, Domine!* the first words of 7:16. The distance between the biblical Job and the reader collapses. As in the Office of the Dead, none of the particulars of Job's case is even mentioned. Initially this makes identification with the reader easier, but the reader soon experiences an analogous erasure. The reader is stripped of all individuating features and replaces them with Job's canonical wish not to be. Right after the certainty of 19:25–27

> I wote ryght well that my Redemptour
> Lyveth yet, and lyve shall aye!
> And I shall ryse, I not what oure,
> Oute of the erthe on Domysdaye,
> And take to me my furst coloure,
> In flesshe and felle, clad on clay.
> And so shall I see my Savyour
> Deme the worlde in wondre aray.

"Pety Job" follows the Office back to the terrors of 10:18:

A, Lord, why leddest Thow so me
Oute of the wombe that I was in?
Wold God I had consumed be
Within myn oune moders skynne!
That the eye with whyche I se
Had nat seyn no more ne mynne![17]

The wish never to have been born was a defining element in the kind of devotion of which "Pety Job" was
a part.[18] "Pety Job" seems a kind of fulfillment of the
wish both to cease to be and yet somehow to survive
oneself in text. Job's book-seeking words at 19:23–24
are part of all these public and private liturgies.

The Books of Hours brought the Office of the
Dead into the home, and into a single person's performance. (It was still, of course, repeated, becoming part of the pious lay person's habitus.) This is
Job without his story, without the friends or Satan
or even God as interlocutor. The Office is still communal, however, mortals consoling and praying for
other mortals, who cower at the rigors of mortal-
ity. Individual devotions following the words of the
Office participated from a distance in this communal ritual. David is near, and Christ is waiting in the
wings. But in adaptations like "Pety Job," Job becomes perhaps for the first time a one-man show,

and so part of the suffering soul's inner monologue in moments of greatest isolation. If the community theater of the Matins of the Office of the Dead showed how much we can and need to do for each other, "Pety Job" and the private devotions made possible by the proliferation of Books of Hours authorized a consciousness of intimate solitude with—or without—God.

Job was a guarantor of individual consciousness, asserting a claim to being on behalf of those whose own words failed. The isolated individual putting on Job's words was not really alone. Job hoped for a *goel*—an advocate, a vindicator (19:25). Here Job was the *goel* advocating for the reader. This advocacy could be understood quite literally, if we recall the veneration of Job as a saint: saints are not merely impressive personages from the past but are viewed as still alive, still able to assist, to intercede.

We have already touched briefly on the cult of Saint Job in connection with more specific ailments. Here a broader and perhaps deeper function of relationships with saints appears. There were few human figures that came closer to the human sufferer than the Job encountered in the Office of the Dead and its offspring. His *was* the human voice addressing the mystery of death. Job continues to have this kind of personal appeal for people who find themselves suffering great and inexplicable sorrow and pain. He cannot perhaps, as his charms once promised, relieve us of leprosy or worms. But Job can give us a template for our grief, transforming experiences of personal eclipse into moments of profoundly human affirmation. Job does more than reassure us that even the saints suffer anguish and inchoate rage. His explosions of grief and despair give hope that our own outbursts may be signs not of weakness but of strength, and even of hope.

Staged Patience

While commentators parsed the arguments of Job and his interlocutors, and while his cries of sublime distress spread from liturgical performance to the theater of private terror and hope, Job's *story* was hardly forgotten. Retold in image, word, and performance, it was an exciting story to tell. It was also a dangerous one. Especially when Job's impassioned words are included, the story's resolution can feel forced. Just who was this God who allowed his most favored servant to be put to such cruel tests? And even if Job's words are inspired, the spectacle surrounding him can make them seem inadequate. Is Job the only one whose ruined life is restored? Is there any hope for all of us who are less favored, and perhaps less faithful, than Job?

A fine example in this respect is the mystery play *La Pacience de Job*, which was performed in French-speaking regions over at least a century and a half into the early seventeenth century.[19] This remarkable work brought together not only the legend of Job and the biblical story, but also the text liturgically celebrated in the Office of the Dead.[20] *La Pacience de Job* exhibits some of the same tensions with the authorized text we encountered already in *Testament of Job*. The story is enhanced with period details and buttressed with biblical parallels. These are surely intended to make Job's exemplary fate stand out, but also have the effect of making the suffering of others more visible.

A single fifteenth-century manuscript of *La Pacience de Job* survives, but printed editions from two centuries later confirm that the play was widely performed. It was a big production, with more than fifty characters. Each of Job's sons and daughters is given a name and a speaking part. Job's servants, herdsmen, and peasants—also named—provide low comedy, while squads of murderous Sabeans and Chaldeans, whipped up by devils, cause mayhem until they turn on each other. Functionaries from the court of Satan appear (one is named Leviathan), held in check by the archangels Gabriel, Raphael, and Michael and the virtues of Hope, Faith, and Patience (an interesting variant on the traditional trio of theological virtues, faith, hope, and charity). A lengthy prologue, invoking Christ and the Virgin Mary, explains the moral of the story: patience is a precious virtue, which allows divine tests to speed us toward eternal happiness. The conduct of Job—the much-afflicted king of Uz in Egypt in this version—is offered for our emulation.

The play opens with a dialogue between two of Job's servants. One complains of his worldly life; his companion replies that he has no hope of a better one. Alongside an extended banquet scene in which Job's sons dine and preach piously about virtue, a peasant dreams of being made a knight but is persuaded by a fellow to accept the wisdom in each man's performing his appointed role. A pastoral diversion, complete with dances and songs, gives way to a scene of Job's shepherds reflecting grimly on the difficult lives of small folk. The scene moves next to the council of devils, where Lucifer orders some lesser devils to lay a trap for God. In the divine court, seen next, God praises Job. When Satan insinuates that Job fears God for naught, God permits the devils to test him. It's a chance for his servant to accrue more virtue.

Job's family and wealth are destroyed in a sequence of grand spectacles. Satan appears in a dream to the king of the Sabeans and convinces him to send an army to rout the dangerous Job—a descendant of Jacob and follower of the Law of

Moses. "If his nation is not destroyed, our law will be done for, very soon overthrown," says the king.[21] Invoking Muhammad (!) he commands a preemptive attack in which many, including the peasant who had complained of his worldly life, are killed. It is the little folk who bring Job the news that the Sabeans, teamed up with the Chaldeans, have made off with his camels and killed his herdsmen, that a fire from heaven has wiped out his sheep, and that all his children are dead.

Job and his wife lament, but while she wishes for death, his grief is heroically measured. As a member of the people of Israel, he reminds his wife of God's testing of Abraham at Moriah.[22] Satan concedes he has lost this round. Meanwhile the heads of the Sabean armies quarrel. Their leader is killed in a duel, his soul eagerly received in hell by devils who waste no time in torturing it. Satan appears once again before God and gets God's permission to attack Job's body. Joined by his superior Lucifer and many other devils, he scourges Job mercilessly, drenching the stage with his blood. Servants take Job to an ash heap while lamenting his downfall in words spoken, in the Bible, by Job himself. Then they abandon him. His wife counsels him to curse God. His friends Eliphat, Baldac, and Sophar engage him in dialogue for a time but drift away when he declares that he knows his savior will vindicate him.

Job Enacted   137

Satan concocts a final and most powerful test. He disguises himself as a beggar, and converts some worms Job has pulled from his body into pieces of gold, which he then shows Job's wife. Persuaded that Job has been hoarding wealth while making her beg, she curses him and leaves. Abandoned by all, Job finally addresses God from the bitterness of his soul, wondering what he could have done to deserve such a fate. God replies with a few rhetorical questions and Job submits in humility and speaks no more. God shares his satisfaction with Job, explaining that he has proved and tested him like fine gold, so that he will be remembered, and be an example to all.[23] God then rebukes Job's friends (Job's words are not commended) and announces to Eliphat that he will restore Job to health and fortune. As the friends assemble materials for Job's sacrifice, the virtues of Faith and Hope intercede on Job's behalf with God, who is happy to accede to their pleas for his "warrior" and "champion."[24] Michael, Gabriel, and Raphael chase Satan away, whom further chastisements await in hell.

Job's life is restored by angels and virtues. Patience, describing herself as "crowned above all the virtues," gives Job a robe and enjoins the spectators to imitate Job in mildly accepting the miseries of life. They should greet the losses God sends them with joy.[25] As the celestial beings return to heaven, Job's friends spread word of his healing. His wife returns, begging forgiveness. Servants, who have likewise returned, dance with Job at his restoration. Before the final customary *Te Deum*, Job's brother, cousin, and sister explain the moral of the story one more time. Only a fool mourns or complains at the miseries of this brief life; the wise cultivate patience as they pilgrim through the "deep abyss" of this world.[26] Job's case shows that God chastises, and then rewards, those he loves, allowing misery to cleanse us of our sins.

La Pacience de Job attests to the persistence and vitality of the legend of Job. (The dimensions of the biblical book are inverted: the events of the frame story, boldly imagined and topically embellished, take up six-sevenths of the play.) With pathos and humor it works out various details of the story, personalizes the herdsmen who are killed, gives the marauding Sabeans and Chaldeans their comeuppance, and brings a kind of balance of cosmic forces by matching the devils with archangels and virtues. The experience of a Europe divided by war is contextualized in a cosmic struggle against Satan—and against his latter day agent, Mohammad.

This Job demonstrates a more convincing patience than the Jobab of *Testament of Job*, who knew too much for his suffering to be more than a test of physical endurance. The protagonist of *La Pacience de Job*, aware of the precedent of the binding of Isaac, suffers in soul as well as body. With echoes of another kind, he uses only those expressions of distress included in the Matins of the Office of the Dead. Performed in the context of Job's history they prove to be miraculously efficacious, eliciting an immediate response from God and the restoration of Job's fortunes. To those familiar with the Office of the Dead, the performance of these David- and Christ-limned words by the hero of this mystery play must have had particular resonance. If Job transforms his own story with these world-transcending words, how much more will they help us transcend our own.

The resolution of *La Pacience de Job* is not quite stable, however. Just as we saw in *Testament of Job*, the writers have not been able to suppress the more dangerous complaints of Job entirely. While Job does not speak them, his bitterest words are displaced onto other characters, whose chorus of complaint about the miseries of human life is not fully silenced by the festivities at Job's restoration. After all, we have been told to find joy in life's miseries, not that we will, like Job, be restored. If we fail we will presumably share the fate of the grumbling peasant. *La Pacience de Job* doesn't just commend patience, but warns against complaint.

Why is there so much complaint among the small folk around Job, however comic? It provides

contrast to Job's patience, but, as we saw in the suffering of Sitidos in *Testament of Job*, the pathos of
the work builds from the realism, not the foolish-
ness, of these dissenting characters. Is Job's example
too hard for most people to hope to follow, or is
the glorious resolution to his story understood to
be too good to be true in a time when many are
suffering depredations like those of Job's servants
and kinsmen? Is the restoration of their king the
best any of his subjects can hope for: does God not
concern himself with the particulars of the lives of
the common folk, whose lot it is to suffer without
grumbling? This was certainly the reality of feudal
Europe, especially in times of war.

In just this context, however, it may be that *La
Pacience de Job* offered a different kind of catharsis.
If grumbling at the evident misery of most human
lives is not permitted in real life, it is permitted in
theater. *La Pacience de Job* offered common folk
who were tempted to grumble a vicarious experience of the articulation of complaint proscribed in
their actual lives. Naming the "deep abyss" of this
world can perhaps wean people from attachment
to the world, reconciling them to the gifts of suffering. It can at the same time also raise suspicions
that God is unjust, and in the shared enactment of
theater, allay them or at least their expression. *La
Pacience de Job* omits much that we believe to be

central to the book of Job, but an appreciation of its dramatic ironies and satisfactions shows that the legend of Job may have effects as complex and troubling as the book of Job itself.

Husbanding Doubt

Could someone watching *La Pacience de Job* have come to the conclusion that God was a moody tyrant concerned only about the powerful, and as a result become an atheist? Writing about the sixteenth-century French world in which *La Pacience de Job* was performed, the historian Lucien Febvre found more skepticism than we might imagine. However, "unbelief" in a modern sense was, he argued, impossible.

> Today we make a choice to be Christian or not. There was no choice in the sixteenth century. One was a Christian in fact. One's thoughts could wander far from Christ, but these were plays of fancy, without the living support of reality. One could not even abstain from observance. Whether one wanted to or not, whether one clearly understood or not, one found oneself immersed from birth in a bath of Christianity from which one did not emerge even at

death. Death was of necessity Christian, Christian in a social sense, because of rituals that no
one could escape, even if one rebelled before
death, even if one mocked and scoffed in one's
last moments.[27]

Febvre overstates the argument for effect, but the
larger point is important. Philosophical and religious positions are not all equally available to all
people at all times. Approaching the problem of
evil in an "aporetic" rather than an "atheistic" way
(as we saw in chapter 2) was often not a deliberate
choice. To a person whose world—natural and su-
pernatural as well as social—is suffused with God,
atheism is not a live option.

"Fools say in their hearts, 'there is no God'"
(Psalm 14:1), but even wise men's hearts aren't im-
mune to doubt. Confidence in the world, its stability
and one's place in it, was something thinkers before
the modern age did not think mortals could achieve
and maintain on their own. Premodern thinkers had
a deeper awareness than we do of how shaky all faith
in knowledge is, just as they had a closer understanding of the mind-deranging effects of pain. Doubt
could not be banished once for all, but it could
be managed. One could preempt it, trapping it in
a ritual sport like *La Patience de Job*, where grumbling, which comes so naturally to fallen people in a

fallen world, is at once allowed to play itself out and curtailed. Philosophers counterposed doubts with other doubts in order to open themselves to insight or support from beyond reason, or at least to allow virtuous habits to hold sway. Only with the rise of modernity will the experience of doubt become potentially liberating. Before this, the question was not whether or not to live with God, but how.

The problem of the compatibility of God and evil is something like the question "should I leave my husband?" The question can in principle be formulated wherever there are marriages. In fact, however, it arises as more than a fancy only where the marital bond is soluble (by the wife) and if there is somewhere within society for a woman to go should she leave her husband. The modern discussion of the problem of evil we will encounter in the next chapter presupposes not only that we are fit to judge the ways of God—indeed to demand a "justification of the ways of God to men"—but that there's something we might *do* about it if we find God's ways unacceptable. Somewhere we might *go*. You can't leave God if he is everywhere, if he is creator and maintainer of everything. The world must seem to have a kind of independent reality if we are to imagine divorcing it from a supposed creator.

This is not the place for an account of how the experience of the world became solid enough that the "atheistic" problem of evil could arise. Premodern struggles with suffering and divine inscrutability are best understood as serious attempts to persist with dignity in a relationship one did not choose, rather than as failures of atheistic nerve. The book of Job and the enactments inspired by it spoke directly to these challenges. Simone Weil, one of the profoundest modern articulators of the depth of premodern understandings, put it well. Job is not a free agent but "struggles like a butterfly pinned alive into an album." Being "nailed down to the spot, only free to choose which way we look" may, however, teach us about our ultimate situation. We may find that we are "nailed to the very center of the universe."[28]

The paradoxes here are explored compellingly in the story of Griselda, a female Job whose widely celebrated suffering and triumph became an "integral part of European culture."[29] It may be that the book of Job has always been about gender. Those interpretations that contrasted Job's steadfast piety with his wife's speaking "as any foolish woman would speak" (Job 2:10) made much of this—even before legend and commentary make her the witting or unwitting agent of Satan. Others, however, noticed that Job's wife suffered all Job did—especially those seeking ways to tell, depict, or act out Job's story. (William Blake, whose *Illustrations of the Book of Job* we consider in the next chapter, made her Job's most steadfast friend.) Patience was at once demanded of women, as for others in subordinate social positions, and thought too much for them to achieve. Meanwhile interpreters, especially those convinced that Job's poetic meter made it a work of epic, had to redefine masculine virtue to render this most passive of biblical heroes a fighter for God.[30]

The story of Griseldis or Griselda tests all these problems at once, from the gendered nature of patience to how to do right in a relationship with an apparently capricious and cruel master. The version of the story that makes up the final tale of Boccaccio's *Decameron* tells of a prince named Walter who takes a poor woman named Griseldis as his wife and puts her through great ordeals to test her obedience to him. Walter takes their children and lets her believe he has killed them, and ultimately tells her she is to be replaced by a nobler bride. In the end, Griseldis' humility and obedience win him over. He declares himself satisfied, and reveals that the children are alive and well. Her obedience wins over the reader, too, who is more than a little disturbed by Walter's behavior. Even if one is put off by her servility, one must surely wonder whether she doesn't deserve a better husband.

Petrarch published a Latin summary of the story under the name "Advice to Wives." In it he introduced an explicit theological moral to what had been a secular tale, and aligned Griselda's story explicitly with Job's. Petrarch shied away from endorsing Walter's behavior, but insisted that Griselda's responses were nevertheless commendable. When he has her say "Naked I came from my father's house and naked I shall return thither," we learn not only that she had the steadfastness of Job but also that the tests through which she had been put were on a Joban scale. Indeed, Petrarch invoked Job to make Griselda an example for us all:

> This story it has seemed good to me to weave anew, . . . not so much that it might stir the matrons of our times to imitate the patience of this wife—who seems to me scarcely imitable—as that it might stir all those who read it to imitate the woman's steadfastness, at least; so that they may have the resolution to perform for God what this woman performed for her husband. For He cannot be tempted with evil, as saith James the Apostle, and He himself tempts no man. Nevertheless, He often proves us and suffers us to be vexed with many a grievous scourge.[31]

The reference to the epistle of James (cf. 1:13) calls to mind James's praise of the "patience of Job."

Petrarch explains that divine tests are for our benefit, that we may know our frailty. (God does not need to test us to know us.) Elsewhere, Petrarch likens Griselda also to the Virgin Mary, another chosen woman of lowly estate, and to Jesus, another victim of public divine scourging. The story's Joban resonances are the strongest, however, and also the hardest to contain. Petrarch concludes that he "would assuredly enter on the list of steadfast men the name of anyone who endured for his God, without a murmur, what this obscure peasant woman endured for her mortal husband."[32]

When Griselda's story is in turn retold by the Clerk of Oxenford in Geoffrey Chaucer's *Canterbury Tales*, the contrast between the angelic heroine and her nearly devilish husband crosses into a criticism of divine callousness. Chaucer's Clerk tells the story he learned from "Frauncys Petrak" (31–32) to respond to a dare: Alison, the Wife of Bath, had charged that no cleric could ever tell a story about a saintly woman (688–91).[33] The story of Job-like Griselda made a doubly appropriate retort, as the Wife of Bath had explicitly invoked the patience of Job for herself, albeit as a suitable quality in husbands (434–41)! Chaucer plays up questions raised in the legend and book of Job about which sex is more patient—but also the question if patience is such a commendable quality after all.

The Clerk's Griselda speaks more than Petrarch's did. Her responses to her trials are exemplary, but she is no automaton of patience. She does not sin with her lips, but her words are double-edged. What seem on the surface to be expressions of devotion at another level suggest terror and a desire for death.

Deth may noght make no comparisoun
Unto your love. (656–57)

For wiste I that my deeth wolde do yow ese,
Right gladly wolde I dyen, yow to plese.
(664–65)

And when Walter tells her he is taking a new and better wife, setting her free, she replies:

God shilde swich a lordes wyf to take
Another man to housbande or to make!
(839–40)

Petrarch explained that Griseldis needed to learn of her own valor, but Chaucer's Griselda needs to learn nothing about herself. If anything, she needs to learn to love a husband who, the Clerk has told us, enjoyed hunting and never wanted a wife in the first place (78–80).

Griselda never complains, but, as we have seen in other adaptations of Job's story, the complaints do not disappear. They are displaced onto other characters. Walter's subjects—whom Walter had told Griselda were unwilling to recognize a commoner as his wife and mother of his children—murmur against his cruelty. Griselda's father, from whose house she came naked in Chaucer as in Petrarch (871–72), curses the day of *his* birth when Walter makes to send her home (902–3). Indeed, the Clerk himself expresses indignation at Walter's acts:

> But as for me, I seye that yvele it sit
> To assaye a wyf whan that it is no nede,
> And putten hire in angwyssh and in drede.
> (459–62)

Chaucer, who makes astute uses of the book of Job elsewhere in the *Canterbury Tales*, finds ways of including reminders of the more challenging parts of the biblical narrative in this tale, too. His Clerk plays up the "merveillous desir" that leads Walter to wish to put Griselda to the test in the first place (454–62), the structural analog to the satan's challenge and wager; he is not master of himself. When Walter reveals to Griselda that it has all been a test and kisses her, she "herde nat what thyng he to hire seyde" but goes into a kind of daze (1058–60). When he indicates that the young woman he'd told her he was to marry in Griselda's stead is in fact their daughter, she faints again. She lives happily ever after, we learn, but a character who had shown herself a mistress of eloquence speaks no more. The two faintings aren't really departures from the Joban template. Structurally they take the place of the divine speeches, though gesturing toward their irrelevance. Griselda's final silence is as strange as Job's.

Meanwhile Chaucer's ending is polyvocal. After Griselda's mute happy end, the Clerk cites Petrarch's conclusion that we should be patient as God pushes no one beyond her limits, but seems unable to endorse it. Griselda's example is now not inimitable but unbearable (1144). And in his telling he has twice used the word "tempt" to describe Walter—a word used in the rest of the *Tales* only in connection with devils (452, 458). A song rounds out the tale, offered by "L'Envoy of Chaucer," which discourages all wives from agreeing to the sort of relationship Griselda had entered into.

Lat noon humylitee youre tonge naille,
Ne lat no clerk have cause or diligence
To write of yow a storie of swich mervaille
As of Griseldis pacient and kynde. (1184–87)

The upshot is deliciously, and disturbingly, multivalent. Petrarch's pious recommendation that all of us should serve God with the patience with which Griselda submitted to Walter's tests is complicated by a Walter who seems not merely capricious but demonic. Perhaps this merely spells out the ways in which the relationship of humans to God is not like that of a wife to a husband or of a subject to a noble lord. But the way Chaucer—no apologist for hierarchy in human life—has let his Clerk tell his tale raises questions about every part of it. People should not put up with the kind of treatment Walter doles out to Griselda. Indeed, they might do well to avoid getting into such relationships entirely, if they can.

Why should anyone accept Walter-like treatment from God? As an Oxford clerk the narrator might have had in mind voluntarist arguments of the sort that will haunt Calvin. God isn't unjust, cruel, or capricious, as Walter was. But he *could* be, with perfect justice. He might do to us what Walter did to Griselda—he did it to Job. It might even be important for us to think of God as a Walter. Petrarch had raised a disturbing question; the answer was disturbing, too. James assures us that God does not need to test us to know our mettle, but we might need testing to understand ourselves. Chaucer's Griselda, however, learns and needs to learn nothing (unless it is to shut her mouth). Walter seems the one convinced and (we hope) transformed. Has not Griselda bested her tester, proving herself the more moral and steadfast? Perhaps the allegory needs to be understood in a different way: "God is to man as Griselda is to Walter."[34]

The Griselda story squirms on the nail of an unchosen relationship to a God whose interest in human beings is ultimately incomprehensible, but which must, somehow, be accepted and welcomed. It names the worries about justice that the book of Job had been naming for centuries, in some ways domesticating them by likening them to long-standing debates about the relationship of the sexes. The story of "patient Griselda" is unappealing to modern readers. She seems to us excessively passive. But Griselda showed a shrewd knowledge of the weapons of the weak, and a growing confidence in the capacities of human character and understanding to hold their own with God.

Job in Theodicy

CHAPTER 4

Religious rivalry and secularization have undermined the authority of scripture, tradition, and
liturgy in the modern West. As a result, new
concerns—theodicy (the problem of evil), ethics, and individual religious experience—have
taken center stage in the practice and the theory
of religion. The book of Job, from its beginnings
something of an outsider to biblical traditions,
played a decisive part in the unfolding of each of
these new emphases, providing crucial templates
and examples. Job legitimated critics of religion
as well as its defenders. It was a book of the Bible,
however, so even as it resonated with challenges
to theological authority, the book of Job helped
the Bible reinvent itself for a new age. As we will
see in this and the next chapter, Job has become
the model of an anguished but fervent modern
religiosity.

Theodicy

Modern religion is constituted by a new set of questions. Central among them is the problem of evil,
given the name "theodicy" in the eighteenth century. Evil and suffering have always been problems,
but theodicy formulates them in a new way. There
is a basic difference between the inquiries into
providence we encountered in Maimonides, Aquinas, and Calvin in chapter 2, and the questions evil
is thought to pose to religion starting in the early
modern period. The premodern wondered *how*
God works in creation, and how the human could
work with God. The modern wonders *whether* God
works in creation at all—and, even if so, whether
this work renders God worthy of worship.

We've seen that one way of appreciating the difference between medieval disputations on providence and modern discourses on theodicy is to
understand the former as "aporetic" and the latter as "atheist" formulations of the question of
God and evil. Like the medieval philosophers,
the eighteenth-century skeptic David Hume gave
the question an ancient, and non-monotheistic,
pedigree:

Epicurus' old questions are yet unanswered.
Is [God] willing to prevent evil, but not able?

then is he impotent. Is he able, but not willing? then is he malevolent. Is he both able and willing? whence then is evil?[1]

The aporetic approach resists these options by seeking ways to reinterpret and reconcile claims about divine attributes and the nature of evil. Cutting the Gordian knot by simply dismissing one of the premises is not an option. In its creative efforts to understand how various authoritative claims can be true together (perhaps evil has an only privative nature? perhaps God cannot know particulars?), this approach has affinities with the ancient interpreters' approach toward scripture. To the atheistic approach to the problem of evil characteristic of modernity, the apparent irreconcilability of these claims suggests that at least one of them is false and should be dismissed. "God and evil?" becomes "God or evil?"

Before the modern period, atheism was not a live philosophical option. In the Psalms, Jewish and Christian readers read of "the fool [who] says in his heart that there is no God" (14:1). Excessive skepticism was understood to be the result of folly, or of sickness. Too much of the black bile that Galenic medicine thought led to melancholy might make a person doubt the existence and meaning of everything—even God. In his famous and influential *Anatomy of*

Melancholy, Robert Burton barely touches on evil in his discussion of religious melancholy. When he does, he doesn't imagine someone might be driven to atheism by the philosophical challenge of evil, but rather the opposite. A person would first have to be mad enough to doubt the existence of God to think the evils in the world could constitute that sort of argument. Martin Luther had the same thing in mind when he described melancholy as "the devil's bath." Even to entertain Epicurus' questions seriously was already a sign of an unhinged mind.

By the end of the seventeenth century, atheism had become more than a figure of speech, though it would be another century before many people openly claimed to be atheists. (Calling your opponents atheists remained the ultimate insult.) Two profound cultural shifts had forced changes in the discussion of providence and human nature. First, the religious wars divided and undermined the authority of churches and with them their interpretations of scripture. Allegorical reading, which we have seen relied on stable ecclesiastical authority, lost credibility. The revival of ancient learning leavened naturalistic understandings of the world and humanity's place in it. A new science of politics emerged that was not premised on original sin and the need for ecclesiastical institutions to deal with it.

Second, the confident discoveries of the scientific revolution led to an enhanced assessment both of human capacities and of the possibility of making a home in this world. The discovery of exceptionless natural laws showed the world to be solid and safe enough for human flourishing. The mechanical philosophy of the seventeenth century rendered all but one of Aristotle's four kinds of causality obsolete. The "efficient causes" so successfully mapped out by modern natural science rendered the "material," "formal," and "final" causes moot. Conceptions of God's relationship to the world changed, and understandings of the agency of those created in the divine image followed suit.

The existential threat of chaos faded along with fear of demonic powers, though not without a struggle. Scientific discoveries did not displace religious faith but reframed it. God worked his wondrous ways through benevolent natural laws. As a result, however, evil—especially human evil—came to be experienced as the inexplicable exception to an otherwise providentially governed world. How could God have permitted it? Paradoxically, evil becomes a discrete philosophical problem as it ceases to be a taken-for-granted and universal experience.

The German philosopher Gottfried Wilhelm Leibniz coined the word "theodicy" in 1710, joining the Greek words for God (*theos*) and justice (*diké*).

His own argument that this must be "the best of all possible worlds" has enjoyed more scorn than approbation in the subsequent history of thought. But the problem now known as theodicy has become centrally important to modern religious life. Leibniz never defined the term, and "theodicy" is now commonly glossed by words from the opening of *Paradise Lost* (1667), where John Milton promised to

assert Eternal Providence,
And justify the ways of God to men. (I.20–24)

By the time Alexander Pope evoked Milton in undertaking to "vindicate the ways of God to men" seventy years later in his philosophical poem *An Essay on Man* (I.16), something important had changed.

Milton's case had been the familiar Christian one. A fallen world had been redeemed by the incarnation, sacrificial death, and resurrection of Jesus Christ. The first man, Adam, learns even before he catapults human beings into sin that his sin will lead to the second Adam, Christ. His fall will thus be a fortunate one. Job is not part of this narrative of the unfolding of Providence. (Job does turn up in the less celebrated sequel, *Paradise Regained*, invoked by *Christ* as an inspiring example!) Whether Milton's justification succeeds is an open question. The

Job in Theodicy   159

Romantic poets famously declared him to be un-
wittingly of the devil's party. In retrospect it seems
that the poetic medium overshadowed the christo-
logical message, or even replaced it. It is now the
task of human art to do the justifying of God's ways.

Alexander Pope's contribution to the discourse
of theodicy, his 1734 *Essay on Man*, drew more on
Lucretius than on biblical narrative, but his work
was understood by many of his contemporaries to
be a philosophical digest and update of God's appearance in the book of Job. Poetic adaptations
especially of the Joban theophany had become an
important literary genre. The climax of Pope's argument brought together popular philosophy, mystery, and art.

> Cease then, nor ORDER Imperfection
>   name:
> Our proper bliss depends on what we blame.
> Know thy own point: This kind, this due degree
> Of blindness, weakness, Heav'n bestows on
>   thee.
> Submit—In this, or any other sphere,
> Secure to be as blest as thou canst bear:
> Safe in the hand of one disposing Pow'r,
> Or in the natal, or the mortal hour.
> All Nature is but Art, unknown to thee;
> All Chance, Direction, which thou canst not see;

All Discord, Harmony, not understood;
All partial Evil, universal Good:

There is only so much that human beings can understand, but Pope hoped through the force of poetry to persuade his readers that it was possible to
make a general affirmation:

And, spite of Pride and erring Reason's spite,
One truth is, "Whatever IS, is RIGHT."
(I.281–94)

There is a vertiginous quality to Pope's language—a
kind of shooting the moon in answer to the problem of evil. Philosophical optimism draws attention
to the very evils it claims to explain away.[2] The template of the Joban theophany requires that one consider not only the morning stars but also the terrible
Behemoth and Leviathan.

The success of the philosophical optimism associated with Leibniz and Pope was not long lasting.
Much more influential was the work of atonement
of a repentant optimist, François Marie Arouet de
Voltaire. The 1755 Lisbon earthquake shook the
French thinker's faith, compelling him to write an
impassioned poem declaring, as if it were news, *il y
a du mal sur la terre!* His famous 1759 novella *Candide* brings together the earthquake and scores of
other evils, acts of men and acts of God. Its vapidly

"candid" protagonist searches for answers for the appalling suffering all around him. His companion, the Leibniz-inspired philosophical buffoon Dr. Pangloss, eventually admits that he's only *saying* that theodicy persuades him. He has in fact "always suffered horribly, but having once affirmed that everything in the world functioned marvelously, he kept affirming it, and never believed it."[3] The closest the protagonists come to an explanation for their sufferings is given by an irritable dervish:

"What difference does it make," said the dervish, "if there is good or evil? When His Highness sends a ship to Egypt, does he worry about whether or not the mice are comfortable on board?"[4]

No definitive interpretation of the meaning of life is required or possible. A better life will be had, Candide finds as the novella comes to its close, if we just "cultivate our garden."

Voltaire's defeat of optimism and its Epicurean moral are a familiar story, but Job's contribution is often overlooked. In Voltaire's response to Pope, we have one modern adaptation of the book of Job responding to another. In a letter to King Frederick the Great of Prussia, Voltaire made it clear: *Candide* was "Job brought up to date."[5] It is the book of Job—in fascinating entanglement with the

Epicurean tradition—which framed the eighteenth century's wrestling with the problem of evil. Job's friends and his wife have fallen out of the picture, as has Satan. The drama now involves the confrontation of a man with God. No mediators, whether covenant or community or Christ, come between them. For Pope, the speech from the whirlwind inspires a paean to a paradoxical universe. For Voltaire, poetry is beside the point—as is the divine poet. Monotheism has imploded. Can there be a more devastating reduction of the Joban theophany than the dervish's ill-tempered words?

Ethics

By the later eighteenth century, the theodicy project of philosophical optimism was dead, but wrestling with the problem of evil was on its way to becoming constitutive of modern consciousness—precisely as a philosophically unsolvable challenge. Faith in God grew not from success in making moral sense of the world but from failure to do so. This was in some ways the return of a premodern view—like the Lutheran view we saw that God had designed the world expressly to drive philosophy to despair. In other ways, however, it was something new, for it established religion not in scripture or sacrament but in consciousness of moral obligation. Central to this transformation was the work of German philosopher Immanuel Kant, whose critical philosophy demolished the foundations of philosophical theology in the 1780s, grounding religion in ethics, and established a new kind of theodicy—with the help of the book of Job—in the 1790s.

It may be surprising to see Kant turn to the book of Job because he had so thoroughly undermined the Bible as a source of authority. Kant had argued that reliance on religious institutions and texts was "heteronomy," a failure to achieve the self-governing "autonomy" befitting a reasonable being. Each person had to legislate the moral law himself. As Kant would argue in his *Religion within the Limits of Reason Alone* in 1792–93, a church or the lessons of scriptures such as the gospels might well be helpful to people in a practical way, buttressing their focus on moral demands. However, the moral law had to come first. The Bible could never be an authority, and certainly no proof text. In the book of Job, however, Kant found something he could use: the story of a man defined by his moral autonomy confronting a God undefined by scripture or ecclesiastical tradition.

Kant's 1791 essay "On the Failure of all Philosophical Essays in Theodicy" is in structure similar to Maimonides' discussion, which we considered in chapter 2. Each begins with a survey of all available philosophical views on their problem and, finding all of them wanting, moves to articulate a kind of "negative wisdom." Kant begins by defining nine possibilities in philosophical theodicy. He reasons that each of the three kinds of problem (sin, pain, and the disproportion between them) can be approached in three different ways (it doesn't really exist, it is an unintended consequence of divine will, it is the result of another will).[6] All prove unconvincing. He concludes that philosophical or "doctrinal" theodicy is impossible. However,

> we cannot deny the name of "theodicy" also
> to the mere dismissal of all objections against
> divine wisdom, if this dismissal is a *divine
> decree*, or (for in this case it amounts to the
> same thing) if it is a pronouncement of the
> same reason through which we form our con-
> cept of God—necessarily and prior to all
> experience—as a moral and wise being. (31)

Kant calls this "authentic theodicy."

Faith in God, Kant had argued in the *Critique of Pure Reason*, may be grounded only in a "moral proof." The world of our experience seems to run on entirely amoral, indeed inhuman, laws. Our moral agency seems to make no dent in it and it is hard not to wonder sometimes if the moral law is just an illusion. To prevent us from dismissing the moral law as a chimera and our freedom as a cruel illusion, we can and must posit a God. Unlike the arguments of the philosophical theodicists, the moral proof is based on the sense of *missing* harmony between the moral and physical worlds. In order that anything make sense, we need to have faith (no knowledge is possible here) in a God who *might* make possible a harmonization of these worlds we cannot ourselves conceive. Belief in a God with any other attributes is no longer permitted. The only argument for the existence of God is what Weber will call the ethical irrationality of the world.

"Authentic theodicy" accepted that the old kind of theodicy was impossible, but could also explain why. Kant's anti-philosophical theodicy is a stance, not an argument: "honesty in openly admitting one's doubts; repugnance to pretending conviction where one feels none" (33). He does not claim to have discovered something new. Indeed, he has found an "authentic interpretation expressed allegorically in an ancient holy book"—the book of Job (32). Job had in fact been the emblem of sincerity for Kant at least since the 1770s.

Kant's Job was a man prosperous, happy, "and on top of all of this (what is most important) at peace with himself in a good conscience" (32). When calamity is sent "in order to test him," he laments to his friends. In the ensuing exchange of theodicies, "each side [speaks] according to its particular way of thinking (above all, however, according to its station)" (32). The friends offer rationalist arguments, Job a more voluntarist one, but what they say is not important. What matters is *how* they say what they say.

> Job speaks as he thinks, and with the courage which he, as well as every human being in his position, can well afford; his friends, on the contrary, speak as if they were being secretly listened to by the mighty one, over whose cause they are passing judgment, and as if gaining his favor through their judgment were closer to their heart than the truth. (32)

Job reproves his friends for the "malice" of presuming to "defend God unjustly" (cf. Job 13:7–11, 16). God knows hypocrites and flatterers and will punish them! God then appears to Job and describes his ways, purposive as well as "counterpurposive." Job "admits having hastily spoken about things which are too high for him and which he does not understand—not *as if wantonly*, for he is conscious of his honesty, but only unwisely" (33). God judges Job's friends; "they have not spoken as well of God as God's servant Job" (ibid.).

Kant's reading of the story stops here. He has already indicated (in a footnote!) that Job isn't entitled to happiness—"one who only does what he owes can have no rightful claim on God's benevolence" (26). Job's example lies in what he does, not what he suffers.

> "Until I die I will not put away my integrity from me, etc." [Job 27:5–6] For with this disposition he proved that he did not found his morality on faith, but his faith on morality: in such a case, however weak this faith might be, yet it alone is of a pure and true kind, i.e. the kind of faith that founds not a religion of supplication, but a religion of good life conduct. (33)

In matters of religion, knowledge is not possible. The best we can do is to be truthful. This includes a recognition of the moral opacity of the world. The idea that religious faith is supported by the experience of providence and design in the world has been turned inside out. The honest religious consciousness admits when things do not make sense. Confident in its moral judgments as well as in its understanding of the natural world, it recognizes the "disproportion between sin and pain" for what it is. It does not cover its eyes or seek special favors, but lives out the destiny of a being of reason and freedom.

In Kant's reading, the book of Job shows that the problem of evil must remain an open wound. The hypocrisy of the God-flattering friends, who claim to see no problem even in Job's innocent suffering, shows the danger of a religion unmoored in morality. The friends aren't really thinking. They haven't even really understood what thinking is. Their "impurity" of heart is what Kant would in *Religion within the Limits of Reason Alone* the next year call the "radical evil in human nature"; lack of clarity about your motives and honesty about the limitations of your human understanding devolve into complete self-deception. Hannah Arendt's "banality of evil" finds its roots in this account. There is an anti-theodicy imperative in the Kantian tradition because human nature is so prone to gloss over the moral paradoxes of existence.

The great Jewish Kantian Hermann Cohen will take this religio-ethical reading of the book of Job one step further. Theodicy of any kind is an offense against not just against God but, even more, against other people. Even supposing there could be a proportion between the merit of human life and action and good or bad fortune is already an ethics-decimating mistake. The encounter with the suffering of the other which Job's friends refused is the start of a true form of existence, but it is rare. Even more precious is its correlate, the assumption of the responsibility for this suffering oneself.

Cohen digs more deeply into Job's recantation and repentance than Kant does. Job doesn't only repent of speaking "unwisely" but drops the whole case, accepting his suffering. The ethical and religious imperative for Cohen becomes the extraordinary claim that, while suffering is not parceled out as punishment for moral transgression, in one's own case it would be good if it were. To Kant's definition of religion as the interpretation of the moral law as divine command, Cohen—inspired by the book of Job—adds that it is the willing of suffering for one's own moral weaknesses. "Suffering is the punishment that man demands inexorably of himself for himself."[7] The Kantian idea that theodicy—and with it the moral or religious interpretation of people's suffering—is the antithesis of ethics remains influential in our own time in the thought of Cohen's successor, Emmanuel Levinas. Levinas appeals to Job in arguing that "the justification of the neighbour's pain is certainly the source of all immorality."[8]

Much of modern religious thought derives from the tension between theodicy and ethics, between the effort to find moral sense in the world and the refusal to accept the world as we find it. Modern thought as a whole can be seen as stemming from the challenge of the problem of evil, from the sense that things are not as they should be.[9] The roles of Job and his friends are often played by ethical critics and religious theodicists, respectively. But religious critiques of the secular theodicies of political economy, philosophy of history, and sociobiology show that the parts can be played the other way, too.

Sublimity

Kant's "authentic theodicy" was only one of several responses to the failure of philosophical theodicy shaped by the book of Job. Others drew on more of the story than Kant did, finding in Job's final words proof that Job's questions could after all be answered—though not in the terms in which they had been posed. The failure of philosophical argument left the individual not alone with his integrity but awed and satisfied by an encounter with a God transcending moral categories. "I have uttered what I did not understand, things too wonderful for me, which I did not know," Job says after God's second speech; "I had heard of you by the hearing of the ear, but now my eye sees you" (42:3, 5). In ways transcending philosophical inquiry, the book of Job *is* a theodicy.

Kant's renegade student J. G. Herder made the claim explicitly:

> The finest descriptions of the attributes and
> of the government of God, the most persua-
> sive grounds of consolation, and whatever can

be said, on opposite grounds of argument, of providence and human destiny are scattered throughout the book [of Job]; but the divinest consolation and instruction are found in the general conception and plan of the book itself.... [I]t is an epic representation of human nature, and a *theodicee* or justification of the moral government of God, not in words, but in its exhibition of events, in that working, that is without words.[10]

The "exhibition of events" Herder praises is the *story* of Job. It involves features of the book of Job which earlier (and later) readers found problematic: what Goethe will call the "prologue in heaven," where God wagers with the satan (1:12, 2:6), and the fact that Job himself never learns of this wager. "Job is made a spectacle to angels and to the whole host of heaven" (I.116). But he is never told of his individual significance, instead finding consolation in a poetic apprehension of the sublimity of God in nature.

Herder traces a poem within the poem of Job, a rising swell of nature poetry given voice first by Bildad (8:9–10, 25:2–6), then by Job (26:2–14), by Elihu (36:22–33, 37:1–12), and finally by God himself (38:2–23, 31–38), passing as it were from mouth to mouth. It cuts across characters and differences of judgment to provide a magnificent tableau of God's providence in nature—and perhaps in the tableau of human types and expressions, too. *We* know that Job suffered for God's honor. *He* knows that God is mighty and wondrous. Divine nature speaks through all. Everyone wins, including poetry.

Approaching the Bible as poetry was part of a reimagining of scripture as a cultural document concurrent with the better-known philosophical movements of the Enlightenment.[11] The Bible, it was increasingly thought, was not philosophy, not a historical chronicle, and certainly not a book of science. It was inspired literature. The appropriate way to understand it was thus not to parse it for arguments or events but to penetrate beyond the surface to the poetic truth at its heart. The book of Job played a central part in this reimagining.

To understand the book of Job as poetry it was not enough to appreciate its beauty and power. One had to know its genre—an ancient question, as we have seen. Jerome had asserted that since it was written in the epic meter of hexameter (it's not), the book of Job must be an epic. This led to centuries of confusion over how a figure who literally did nothing could be the hero of an epic. Allegory came to the rescue. Job's words were like the sparks flying from a pitched battle against Satan. Patience was perhaps the most difficult part of the virtue of fortitude.

In the 1740s, Robert Lowth succeeded in articulating the distinguishing character of biblical poetry—the structure of intensifying pairs of lines known as "parallelism." This marked a major event in the history of biblical scholarship; at the same time it marked the emergence of the modern concept of literature as its own sphere of human creativity expressing most profoundly the relation of the human to transcendent questions. If the Bible could be poetry, poetry could be sacred. The book of Job inspired Lowth's project, and was his first illustration of the sublimity definitive of what he called the "sacred poetry of the Hebrews."[12]

The description of the war horse in Job 39:19–25 was a celebrated model of the sublime, but Lowth, following Longinus, declared himself interested in something more profound:

> I speak not merely of that sublimity, which exhibits great objects with a magnificent display of imagery and diction; but that force of composition, whatever it be, which strikes and overpowers the mind, which excites the passions, and which expresses ideas at once with perspicuity and elevation. (2:307)

Lowth directed attention to the curses of Job 3. He noticed that Job seems to interrupt himself, switching abruptly from first to second person—just as one who truly spoke from "violent affection" would. For Lowth this was the hallmark of Hebrew poetry, and its gift and challenge to those who came later and spoke less raw languages. While later refinements made poetry more artful, the Bible exemplified in its truest form the power and aim of poetry: "it insinuates or instils into the soul the very principles of morality itself" (1:35–37).

Following Jerome, Lowth argued that the categories of ancient literary criticism could help one appreciate what the Bible was up to. Biblical poetry met and surpassed the requirements of all the genres: elegiac, didactic, lyric, idyllic, and dramatic. The book of Job should be understood as drama. While there is no "action" in Aristotle's sense, the book of Job is supremely about the testing of character. It shows that even the noblest soul, when pushed to its limits, will move to desperate words (2:378). Yet so true do these words ring—Job and his friends speak exactly as the occasion dictates (2:393)—that we excuse them: "those vehement and perverse attestations of his innocence, those murmurs against the divine Providence, which his tottering virtue afterwards permits, are to be considered merely as the consequences of momentary passion" (2:410).

Aristotle had deemed the suffering of a truly good person to be a subject unsuitable for drama, but that just showed the limitations of one unexposed to the grandeur of biblical poetry.

> This opinion of the philosopher seems to result from an unjust and visionary estimation of human virtue, to repress which appears to have been the very design and object of the book of Job. The character of Job indeed, though approaching so near to the perfection of virtue, seems, notwithstanding, to have a considerable alloy of human infirmity, so as neither to want probability, nor to lose its effect in exciting terror. For if it be extreme wickedness in the most upright of men, when oppressed with the severest misery, to murmur at all against the divine justice, who then shall stand before God?
> (2:416–17)

The book of Job teaches us that the drama of virtue affronted is perhaps the profoundest subject of all. Its plot is the turning and correcting of such a noble character. The dialogue with the friends "is not more than an instrument of temptation, and is introduced in order to explain the inmost sentiments of Job, and to lay open the latent pride that existed in his soul" (2:396). Lowth spends almost no time on the theophany; Job's arrival at readiness to hear God is more important than what God says. The book of Job's truth lay not in extraordinary prophetic foreknowledge—Lowth thought 19:25–27 did not "contribute in the least to the main design of the Poem, nor to be consistent with the object of it" (2:357, 386–7). Its sacred gift lay in the powerful human feelings it expressed and evoked.

As Enlightenment gave way to Romanticism, the book of Job came more and more to be seen as the portrait of God in his sublimity. Enlightenment thinkers thought religion must be rational or pass away, but Romantic examinations of the range of human experience found new ways of understanding the significance of religion. On the cusp of the nineteenth century, Friedrich Schleiermacher introduced the influential idea that religion's heart was experience, not doctrine or ethics. Specifically, religion was an experience of absolute dependence, of being acted on. Yet this experience of passivity was one in which agency was not lost but found, an experience not disturbing and disempowering but comforting and exalting.

The book of Job was never far from these discussions. A particularly striking articulation of its significance appears in Christian theologian and scholar of comparative religion Rudolf Otto's *The Idea of the Holy* (1917), which argues that God's speeches constitute a true theodicy. What vindicates God is not the story of the book of Job but the creation described by the creator to his creature, Job. Job is appeased and repents in dust and ashes, consoled and reconciled.

How is Job consoled and reconciled? The presentation of pleasing purposiveness so important for Herder has vanished. God presents the firmament and the foundations of the earth, but is most compelling in his accounts of the eagle, ostrich, unicorn, crocodile, and hippopotamus.[13] These are hardly examples one would choose in trying to demonstrate the purposiveness of creation, Otto observes. Instead, they are marvels, more monstrous than magnificent, and testify to the *mysteriousness* of God. What might the ostrich, for instance, suggest about the creator who describes it?

> The ostrich's wings flap wildly,
>> though its pinions lack plumage.
> For it leaves its eggs to the earth,
>> and lets them be warmed on the ground,
> forgetting that a foot may crush them,
>> and that a wild animal may trample them.
> It deals cruelly with its young, as if they were
>> not its own;
>> though its labor should be in vain, yet it has
>> no fear;
> because God has made it forget wisdom,
>> and given it no share in understanding.

When it spreads its plumes aloft,
it laughs at the horse and its rider. (39:13–18)

In God's speeches to Job from the whirlwind, Otto asserts, "we have the element of the mysterious displayed in rare purity and completeness."[14] *Mysterium* is part of Otto's account of the experience of the holy, the "numinous," which he claims is the "non-rational" element in religion, older and deeper than the rational. The other elements of the *mysterium tremendum et fascinans* are terror and attraction.

Otto insists that God's speech in the book of Job offers a "real theodicy . . . able to convict even a Job, and not only convict him, but utterly still every inward doubt that assailed his soul" (78). He is less clear about the nature of this conviction. In response to the divine speeches Otto finds that "Job avows himself to be overpowered, truly and rightly overpowered, not silenced by superior strength." His repentance in dust and ashes is not "impotent collapse and submission to merely superior power" but an "admission of inward *convincement* and conviction" (78). "*Convincement*"? The translator struggles with the near-neologism in Otto's original German, *Überführt-seins*, a term suggesting a state of being outdone, overtaken, swept into assent.

Otto's accounts seem to protest too much. Each one is shadowed by the very bullying from which

Job in Theodicy   179

Otto distinguishes it. Yet he knows what he's doing. What happens to Job, what Job's words report, is not a rational conviction but another kind, and can barely be expressed in words. While crucially different from a humiliating show of force, it is still closer to that than to the satisfactions of discourse. Otto can't tell us what makes it convincing, only *that* Job is convicted, convinced. The best he can do is make the point indirectly through a form of writing which partakes of the tradition of the sublime. This is a theodicy, but not one that human words can convey:

> [T]he *mysterium* . . . live[s], not in any explicit concepts, but in the tone, in the enthusiasm, in the very rhythm of the entire exposition. . . . That of which we are conscious is rather an *intrinsic value* in the incommensurable with thoughts of rational human teleology and is not assimilated to them: it remains in all its mystery. But it is as it becomes felt in consciousness that Elohim is justified and at the same time Job's soul brought to peace. (80)

Otto's ideas live on in the field of the history of religions. He was praised by Mircea Eliade among others for using the comparative method to establish something universal at the heart of all religious experience, something beyond the level of thought

but still recognizable and theorizable. Another legacy is the evocative character of Otto's writing—
something he draws from traditions of apologetics but also from the demands of the sublime.[15]
The non-rational cannot be spoken of in normal
language.

The missionary aspirations of religious studies
have been curbed in recent years, but the claims of
some kinds of philosophy and literary theory now
go where angels fear to tread. Otto's prolific contemporary, G. K. Chesterton, penned a character-
istically luminous introduction to an edition of the
Book of Job in 1916, echoing central themes of his
Orthodoxy. For Chesterton the book of Job dares,
as no other book of the Old Testament does, to ask,
"what is the purpose of God? Is it worth the sacrifice even of our miserable humanity? Of course it
is easy enough to wipe out our own paltry wills for
the sake of a will that is grander and kinder. But is
it grander and kinder?"[16] The book of Job answers
these questions as Chesterton insists one must answer all doubters—by upping the ante:

In dealing with the arrogant asserter of doubt,
it is not the right method to tell him to stop
doubting. It is rather the right method to tell
him to go on doubting, to doubt a little more, to
doubt every day newer and wilder things in the

universe, until at last, by some strange enlightenment, he may begin to doubt himself. (xxi)

The significance of Job, Chesterton insists, is that
he is "suddenly satisfied with the mere presentation of something impenetrable . . . He has been
told nothing, but he feels the terrible and tingling
atmosphere of something which is too good to be
told" (xxi). Indeed, the lesson of the book of Job as a
whole is that "man is most comforted by paradoxes"
(xxvii). In *Orthodoxy*, Chesterton had ventured that
the attempt to be entirely reasonable is itself a form
of insanity. It is a part of sanity to accept mystery.

> God will make Job see a startling universe if
> He can only do it by making Job see an idiotic
> universe. To startle man God becomes for an
> instant a blasphemer; one might almost say that
> God becomes for an instant an atheist. (xxiii)

Chesterton's pithy profundities on the topic of
Job have recently received a second life through
the attention of philosopher Slavoj Žižek, a Christian atheist—someone who thinks that the truest
account of the riddle and challenge of living and
thinking may be that of a Christian theology un-
burdened by faith in an actual God.[17]

Understanding the book of Job as sublime can
mean the displacement of God by poetry and

paradox, which express the indomitability of the human spirit on its own. But it can also focus on the bridging of disjunctive realities through relationship. God deigns to speak to one of his creations, and for once he does not talk down to him. The encounter affirms in performance the commensurability it otherwise seems to call into question. The suffering Job's questions are not addressed in the theophany. He is.

Vision

Job's experience of convincement is perhaps best represented by images, not words. An account of Job's place in modern life and imagination would not be complete without a discussion of the *Illustrations of the Book of Job* by William Blake. Blake has come to own Job the way Michelangelo owns the creation of man and Leonardo the Last Supper, but few understand all that Blake meant by his cycle of images. The cycle is more premodern and also more psychological, more mythological and more personal, than anything imagined by Enlightenment philosophers or poets. It is also more theological, a reminder that the Christian tradition has inspired mystics and revolutionaries as well as systematizers and reformers. Genuine Christianity, for

Blake, must move beyond the hearing of the ear to a true seeing of the eye, a point Blake found was made in the book of Job with particular force—and in a story that in turn demanded to be told in image, not just in word.

Blake's illustrations call to us from the covers of books not only on Job but on the problem of evil. The destruction of Job's sons by a collapsing building, beneath a terrifying bat-winged Satan, graces the cover of Oliver Leaman's *Evil and Suffering in Jewish Philosophy*. The fingers of Job's accusing friends, splayed like a winnowing comb, front many books, including Bruce Zuckerman's *Job the Silent* and Robert Alter's recent translation of *The Wisdom Books*. God's appearance to Job in a whirlwind, his arms outstretched, is the face not just of the collection of Blake's work edited by Harold Bloom but of several psychoanalytic studies of the self. It appears also on the cover of a collection of Kenzaburo Oe's essays on Hiroshima. The parade of the morning stars fronts both Stephen Mitchell's poetic version of Job and the fiftieth anniversary edition of Jung's *Answer to Job*. Behemoth and Leviathan, rolled up in a ball, appear as covers of works from psychology to science fiction. Raymond Scheindlin's poetic translation of the book of Job, first published with a medieval image on its cover, ended up with Blake's engraving of Job praying for his friends.

Blake's cycle of twenty-one images, originally a series of watercolors painted in 1805–10 and amplified and engraved as a series in 1825, seems at first sight to tell the familiar biblical story. (In recent years the watercolors have become better known than the engravings, but it is the latter that Blake intended for circulation.) Job begins and ends surrounded by children and sheep. Satan appears before the divine court a dashing dark figure, and is given permission to destroy Job's sons and flocks and to attack his body. The friends arrive, their arms thrown up in distress on first seeing their blighted friend but soon outstretched in accusation. When God appears they cover their faces, the whirlwind seeming to press them into the ground. After God shows the wonderful and the terrible in creation in beautifully composed tableaux, Job is reconciled, conducts a sacrifice for his friends, and the story ends with Job again in the bosom of his family. Given a kind of timeless mythological power by Michelangeloan physiques and landscapes of Druidic, gothic, and classical architecture, the images stand at just the right remove from traditional representations of biblical history to be accessible across time.

Blake's story also has some unusual emphases. There are two dream sequences—Eliphaz' dream and Job's night torment, when a wild-haired figure with a hoofed right foot and a serpent entwining his legs presses down on Job as hands reach up from below to pull him down. When Job sees the true God it seems to be a figure like Christ holding his arms out in blessing over Job and his wife (see figure 8). Indeed, breaking with all traditions of interpretation and depiction, in Blake's vision Job's wife is his most loyal friend. She is by his side throughout and, uncowed, she sees God when he does. Musical instruments that had been hung in the oak tree overhead in the opening scene, judged inappropriate to piety, are being played in the final scene as the company joyously stands. It's a restoration but also a reconciliation of different parts of life, the restoration of art to worship, creativity to religion. Most striking, Job's face and the faces of God are the same.

Many of these themes have analogues in other works of Blake, whose publications can all be seen as expressions of a single dominating vision. To those familiar with the "prophetic books" *Milton* and *Jerusalem*, especially, Blake's story of Job will seem very familiar. Job looks like Albion, the protagonist of *Jerusalem*, and his old god looks like blind Urizen, the face of reason and also of the illusions of time and space. Albion suffered Job-like setbacks, too, driving his children away through a narrowly judgmental religion. Both protagonists first suffer under a deity projected from their own moralism, then have a turnaround that opens their

Figure 8. William Blake's *Illustrations of the Book of Job* set scenes inspired by the book of Job in elaborate frames of symbols and biblical text, inverting the traditional relationship of text and illustration. To 42:5 ("I had heard of you by the hearing of the ear, but now my eye sees you") Job and his wife see a God who looks a lot like Christ (and like Job), as his friends cower to the side.

eyes to the wonder of existence and to their own nature as godlike in divine humanity.

The dream in which Job writhes in anguish under the satanic-looking God closely resembles an older image of the creation of Adam which looks more like binding. In an almost Gnostic way, Blake saw the creation as a painful insertion into the illusory realities of flesh and gender, space and time— the pernicious myths especially of the modern age and its monstrous "natural religion." Meanwhile, the young, vigorous Satan reminds us of the Satan of *Milton*, whose namesake and hero seemed of the devil's party unwitting.

As one pursues the antecedents to the figures, layouts, and symbols of the *Illustrations of the Book of Job*, it can start to seem that Blake isn't really interested in Job at all. There is only one religion, and Job is being fit into it. Yet Job had been a preoccupation of Blake's for a very long time. And on closer study, the Job illustrations prove to be astonishingly faithful to commentarial and even visual traditions of Job interpretation, even in elements that strike us as capricious. For instance, the instruments in the trees evoke Psalm 137:2 and the Babylonian captivity, the time when many scholars thought the book of Job had been written. The Druidic elements of Job's sacrifices draw on an understanding, shared by many radical thinkers of Blake's day, that the

Druids were contemporaries and kin of the biblical patriarchs.[18]

The frames Blake designed for the publication of his engravings make clear how profoundly steeped he was in the Bible. They incorporate line-drawn symbols showing the flow of the story—serpents' scales presaging satanic appearances, a forest of errors growing, only to be blown down by a whirlwind, symbolic animals and plants, and a broken pot just in time for Job to scratch his boils. Interwoven with these are scores of quotations from the Bible in scrolls, books, and skeins of words. The text-laden frames invert the structure and logic of a traditional illuminated Bible. The words "gloss the images rather than vice versa."[19] Much of the book of Job appears in these frames. Every passage that has been the hinge of an important reading is included, with the revealing exception of 28:28's "the fear of the Lord, that is wisdom; and to depart from evil is understanding."

It is an explicitly Christian project, in ways one might have thought spent or lost by Blake's time. Ranging from Genesis to Revelation, Blake's intertextual nods and prods convey a countercultural understanding of the book of Job that is prophetic and even typological—though with a twist. Job in extremis discovers the true God, the God of forgiveness, and so rediscovers or reconnects with the divine human nature. Blake's radical ideas were not orthodox, but they were serious and seriously Christian. One recent theological analysis of the problem of innocent suffering has argued that Blake's vision of the book of Job "reflects fully the stream of tradition which had preceded it" and manages to express an understanding uniquely suited to modern forms of faith. We see "experience as no longer directly engineered by God" and find the divine instead in creative subliming of otherwise meaninglessly general experience.[20]

The program of the engravings is made clear by the words engraved on an altar at the bottom of the first plate: "The Letter Killeth / The Spirit giveth Life and they are spiritually discerned."[21] All of Blake's works are lessons in discernment, in how to see true reality beyond the illusions of space and time, the natural religion and moral law characteristic of his age. The epistle of James's reference to the *patience of Job* attends the scene of the arrival of Job's friends, balancing "What! Shall we recieve (sic) Good at the hand of God & shall we not also recieve Evil." Provocatively and profoundly, Job arrives at the confidence that his "Redeemer liveth" in the frame below the image of his dream of a demonic god. The God of the morning stars is the creator of the world: scenes of the six days of creation from Genesis flank the image.

Around the image of Job (and his wife) seeing a Christlike God, an image added when Blake
adapted the series for engraving, we find a flurry
of Johannine texts, in books as well as scrolls. "We
know that when he shall appear we shall be like him
for we shall see him as He Is; He that hath seen me
hath seen my Father also; I & my Father are one"
and most of the fourteenth chapter of John culmi-
nating in "At that day he shall know that I am in
my Father, and ye in me, and I in you."[22] The figure of a man with arms outstretched is repeated in
the next scene where Job prays for his friends—*his*
arms now spread as in crucifixion; a book opens to
the fifth chapter of Matthew: "I say unto you / Love
your En/emies bless them that curse you, do good
to them that hate you, and pray for them which de-
spitefully use you, and persecute you . . ." Job has
learned that his nature is divine, that the sacrifice
of Christ has made it possible for him to transcend
the self imposed if inevitable errors of materialism
and moralism. "For Blake, no one can 'see' God
until God becomes a human being," Northrop Frye
wrote, "and even then he is not so much what we see
as what we see with."[23]

We are only able to scratch the surface of the
involved structures that have been discerned in
the imagery and sequence of Blake's *Illustrations*.
Blake intended the engravings to be accessible to a

public uninitiated in the world of his other work. Clearly they are still compelling. As an interpretation of the biblical book, Blake's cycle is faithful in unexpected and often revealing ways. Job truly sees God in his flesh, so it is literally true when he says, "I had heard of you by the hearing of the ear, but now my eye sees you" (42:5). Blake also finds a way to include the wager in heaven, and even to make sense, as only the ancient rabbis had before him, of Satan's roaming about on earth before that. What instigates Job's whole trial is the doubt raised by his own anxiously self-righteous sense of godliness. Satan is able to come from the space between man and God because Job has allowed such a gulf, even as he thinks he has closed it through piety.

Blake's view of the book of Job as the story of a soul, overcoming its own barriers to understanding self and world, may seem to dodge the theodicy question just as its premodern precursors had done. Is evil only an illusion? Blake had a theodicy of his own, famously articulated in "The Marriage of Heaven and Hell":

Without Contraries is no progression. Attraction and Repulsion,
Reason and Energy, Love and Hate, are necessary to Human existence.

From these contraries spring what the religious
   call Good & Evil.

Good is the passive that obeys Reason. Evil is
   the active springing from Energy. . . .

That theodicy is enacted in the *Illustrations of the
Book of Job*, and grounded in the biblical text. It is
Job's very "eschewing of evil" that provokes his crisis. He suffers because of his refusal to acknowledge
the creativity of evil. But Blake's story doesn't touch
the questions the book of Job raises about the apparent injustice of human life and of the God who
acts in it. All the suffering in Blake's story is the result of Job's journey toward a truer understanding
of divine and human nature. God is off the hook.
At the same time, Blake comes close to reviving the
Gnostic claim that the world of suffering is so awful
that it can only be seen as the work of an evil god
and those in his thrall.

It is doubtful that the many users of Blake's *Illustrations* endorse or even recognize Blake's personal,
aesthetic, and in its distinctive way very Christian
theodicy. What speaks most clearly from these images is their saturated and strange visuality itself,
the expression of an experience of the world, the
soul, and God that pushes words to the margins. It
might be argued that Blake's wild artistic liberties,
flouting the false modern pieties of the natural, the

reasonable, and the moral, are what recommend these images as definitive for us. As Blake would affirm, everyone sees the world differently. The book of Job, more than any other work, needs to be discerned and expressed anew by each person.

Job in Exile

Thus far I have made a point of talking about the book of Job as a unified text. This is the way every book of the Bible was understood until modern historical critical scholarship changed our understanding of scripture. Earlier interpreters noticed oddities and tensions that we now attribute to multiple or even competing authorships, but that interpretive option was not open to them. The legacy of the ancient interpreters who made the Bible the Bible continued to inform these readings, whether one was a member of an interpretive community that worked hard to excise even the appearance of ambiguity, or one that rejoiced in ambiguity as an invitation to dig deeper. The kinds of reading that thrived on these strategies progressively lost credibility in the modern age, however, especially among Christians.

This chapter follows the book of Job through the upheavals of the twentieth century. Interpreters

scrambled to make sense of historical critical discoveries, daring for the first time explicitly to edit
the book of Job in small and large ways. Many have
come to the view that the "first thing you need to
know about the Book of Job is that there are two of
them"[1]—the frame story and the poem—and that
we have to choose between them. This was also the
century in which historical horrors and the emergence of a "Judeo-Christian tradition" led both
Jews and Christians to see Job as essentially Jewish
for the first time. As the purest expression of the
drama of a transcendent monotheism, the book of
Job came to be seen as one of the truest depictions
of the struggles of faith.

Textual Troubles

A new way of reading the Bible emerged with
modernity, inspired by the Renaissance human-
ists' philological discoveries regarding the texts
of Greco-Roman antiquity. The search for an authoritative text from among several often widely
varying manuscripts led eventually to questions
about variations within the texts themselves. The
Reformation's commitment to the sufficiency of
scripture (*sola scriptura*) required precise editions
and translations. Seventeenth-century writers like

Baruch Spinoza, Thomas Hobbes, and Richard Simon started reading the Bible as one might read any other ancient text, inquiring after the historical contexts in which it was written and the vicissitudes of its history of transmission. Questions of this sort had been asked before; Spinoza's work was inspired by the example of the twelfth-century ibn Ezra, for instance. Yet the intention had changed in ways parallel to the transformed engagement with evil chronicled in the last chapter. The question was no longer what the text had to say to the present but whether or not the text was reliable, and whether it had anything to say to us at all.

Historical critical biblical scholarship, beginning in earnest in German Protestant universities in the nineteenth century, took this approach to a new level. This way of studying the Bible was as much the child of the Enlightenment's commitment to critique all claims to authority as of Romanticism's fascination with origins and works of genius. Its most famous fruit was the "documentary hypothesis" associated with Julius Wellhausen, which explained repetitions, parallels, and apparent contradictions in the texts of the first six books of the Hebrew Bible by seeing it as a work with several layers of editing. The chronology proposed has been contested—it has an anti-Jewish slant consistent with enduring Christian prejudices about supposed

Jewish "ritualism"—but not the underlying idea. The texts of the Bible are not simply the outpouring of inspired individuals. The texts as we receive them have been worked over by different authors and editors working in different contexts, possibly with different agendas. This need not spell the end of the Bible as revelation, of course. If God could inspire a poet in the wilderness, God could also guide a committee of editors in the city.

What of the book of Job? Text-critical interpretation had delivered the conclusion that the book of Jeremiah was originally the work of a poet; its prose sections were deemed a later addition. Was the relationship of the poetic and prose sections of Job perhaps analogous? Could it have been written all at once by a single author? If not, did the author of the poem come first, or the author of the prose frame story? Who were these authors, and what were they up to? In line with the Romantic conviction that poetry was older and purer than prose, the earliest theories positing multiple authorship asserted that the poem of Job must have been first. This account was inverted in the final quarter of the nineteenth century. Few now doubt that the pious tale of Job preexisted the text in some (probably oral) form, but the actual language of the prose frame is archaizing rather than archaic, and could well have been written *after* the poet wrote. In time, analysis of language, structure, and meaning made clear that the book of Job is an even more compli-cated composite.

The book of Job's frame story and the poetic di-alogues are disjoint on many levels. The language is qualitatively different—one not just poetry but sublime, the other not only prose but spare and stylized in the manner of a folk tale. Even God is re-ferred to by different names. What is more, there is no reference to the events of the prose frame in the poem. The satan, who never appears in the poem, disappears even from the prose epilogue. Most troublingly, it can seem that two entirely different Jobs are described. One is a man of few—perhaps only proverbial—words; in the epilogue he doesn't speak at all. The other overflows with words.

Was the poem written in righteous indignation or savage parody to turn a pious tale inside out, a test by God transformed into a trial *of* God? It is possible to reconstruct the kind of dialogue that would have taken place between Job and his friends in the prose story before it was interrupted. The friends were presumably as feckless as Job's wife and elicited similarly stalwart responses from an unmovable Job—along with the divine reprimand they deserved for their fickleness. We can imagine that this saccharine tale provoked an intervention from a brilliant poet whose eyes had been opened to God's inscrutable ways and to the hollowness of standard formulas of piety.

Or was the poem there first, the frame story slapped on later to contain a dangerous text that was too celebrated to be ignored? The Song of Songs may have found its way into the canon of scripture this way, a cooptation where suppression failed that led to some of the most inspiring understandings of divine love in biblical traditions.[2] If the frame of the book of Job was designed to limit the threat posed by the poem, it succeeded in its aim for several millennia, although, as we have seen, it also allowed the incen-diary clarity of the poetic Job to enrich and deepen human experiences of confusion and unjust suffering.

Whatever the intentions of the writers of the prose and poetic parts of Job, the resulting text stimulates profound reflections on the nature of piety and patience. Indeed, its apparently disparate parts accomplish this so well that one recent inter-preter has suggested they might be the work of one brilliant writer after all, inspired by the difficulty of the questions raised by the story of Job to produce a mixed text out of well-known but conflicting genres. Its "polyphony" prevents any one of its voices from having the last word, and so ensures that the work of questioning (and answering) goes on.[3]

The cycle of dialogues between Job and his friends presents textual incongruities, too. Job addresses the friends' arguments belatedly if at all. Their views even seem in a few places to be mistakenly put in Job's mouth. Structurally the series of speeches seems compromised, too. Bildad's third speech is so short it seems cut off, and Zophar has no third speech at all. The next very long set of speeches (Chapters 25–31) is evidently delivered by Job, but these speeches hardly seem to flow from the same voice. Chapter 27, for instance, sounds much more like the position of the friends than anything Job has said. Job's speeches are often full of bitter parodies of other people's language, but this speech lacks clear signs of irony.

Synthesizing the most persuasive suggestions about how to understand and remedy these dislocations, the doyen of Job scholars recommended a significant rearrangement of texts:

> [T]he simplest and most satisfactory expedient is to augment Bildad's abbreviated discourse of xxv with the beautiful paean to God's power in xxvi 5–14 and to supply the missing speech of Zophar from the incongruous parts of Job's speech, xxvii 8–23, to which may be added appropriately xxiv 18–20, 22–25.[4]

These suggestions are powerfully argued on philological grounds and are widely followed. (The *Jewish Study Bible* mentions them but suggests another view: see figure 9.) A recent poetic translator thinks it better to give up Zophar's last speech for lost.[5] Yet there are other ways of interpreting the truncation of the cycle of speeches. One could also see the collapse of the cycle of speeches as a way of conveying the exhaustion of the topic.[6] The words put in Job's mouth in Chapter 27 could be confirmation of that—precisely as a pitch-perfect articulation of the friends' views. He knows their views inside out. He can even express them more forcefully than they. But the words have become hollow. The following chapter, which eloquently describes the inaccessibility of wisdom, might flow from just such a catharsis.

Chapter 28, the "Hymn to Wisdom," raises questions of its own. Who exactly is speaking, and to whom is it addressed? This speech approaches questions about wisdom nobody has asked. In the absence of indications to the contrary, the speaker would seem still to be Job. However, the speech of Chapter 29 is introduced with the words, "Job again took up his discourse and said . . . ," suggesting that someone else had just been speaking. If it is Job, he seems a changed man. If he has such a philosophical view, the rest of the book seems quite unnecessary. Chapter 28 seems like an independent work, an interlude taken from another context entirely. It may even predate the rest of

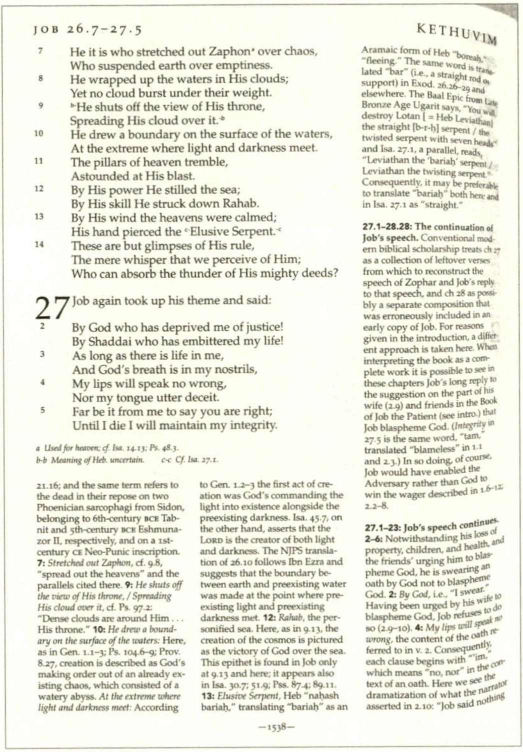

JOB 26.7–27.5 KETHUVIM

7 He it is who stretched out Zaphon[a] over chaos,
Who suspended earth over emptiness.
8 He wrapped up the waters in His clouds;
Yet no cloud burst under their weight.
9 [b]He shuts off the view of His throne,
Spreading His cloud over it.[b]
10 He drew a boundary on the surface of the waters,
At the extreme where light and darkness meet.
11 The pillars of heaven tremble,
Astounded at His blast.
12 By His power He stilled the sea;
By His skill He struck down Rahab.
13 By His wind the heavens were calmed;
His hand pierced the [c]Elusive Serpent.[c]
14 These are but glimpses of His rule,
The mere whisper that we perceive of Him;
Who can absorb the thunder of His mighty deeds?

27 Job again took up his theme and said:
2 By God who has deprived me of justice!
By Shaddai who has embittered my life!
3 As long as there is life in me,
And God's breath is in my nostrils,
4 My lips will speak no wrong,
Nor my tongue utter deceit.
5 Far be it from me to say you are right;
Until I die I will maintain my integrity.

a Used for heaven; cf. Isa. 14.13; Ps. 48.3.
b-b Meaning of Heb. uncertain. *c-c Cf. Isa. 27.1.*

21.16; and the same term refers to the dead in their repose on two Phoenician sarcophagi from Sidon, belonging to 6th-century BCE Tabnit and 5th-century BCE Eshmunazor II, respectively, and on a 1st-century CE Neo-Punic inscription. **7:** *Stretched out Zaphon*, cf. 9.8, "spread out the heavens" and the parallels cited there. **9:** *He shuts off the view of His throne, / Spreading His cloud over it*, cf. Ps. 97.2: "Dense clouds are around Him . . . His throne." **10:** *He drew a boundary on the surface of the waters:* Here, as in Gen. 1.1–3; Ps. 104.6–9; Prov. 8.27, creation is described as God's making order out of an already existing chaos, which consisted of a watery abyss. *At the extreme where light and darkness meet:* According to Gen. 1.2–3 the first act of creation was God's commanding the light into existence alongside the preexisting darkness. Isa. 45.7, on the other hand, asserts that the LORD is the creator of both light and darkness. The NJPS translation of 26.10 follows Ibn Ezra and suggests that the boundary between earth and preexisting water was made at the point where preexisting light and preexisting darkness met. **12:** *Rahab*, the personified sea. Here, as in 9.13, the creation of the cosmos is pictured as the victory of God over the sea. This epithet is found in Job only at 9.13 and here; it appears also in Isa. 30.7; 51.9; Pss. 87.4; 89.11. **13:** *Elusive Serpent*, Heb "naḥash bariaḥ," translating "bariaḥ" as an Aramaic form of Heb "boreaḥ," "fleeing." The same word is translated "bar" (i.e., a straight rod or support) in Exod. 26.26–29 and elsewhere. The Baal Epic from Late Bronze Age Ugarit says, "You will destroy Lotan [= Heb Leviathan] the straight [b-r-ḥ] serpent / the twisted serpent with seven heads" and Isa. 27.1, a parallel, reads, "Leviathan the 'bariaḥ' serpent / Leviathan the twisting serpent." Consequently, it may be preferable to translate "bariaḥ" both here and in Isa. 27.1 as "straight."

27.1–28.28: The continuation of Job's speech. Conventional modern biblical scholarship treats ch 27 as a collection of leftover verses from which to reconstruct the speech of Zophar and Job's reply to that speech, and ch 28 as possibly a separate composition that was erroneously included in an early copy of Job. For reasons given in the introduction, a different approach is taken here. When interpreting the book as a complete work it is possible to see in these chapters Job's long reply to the suggestion on the part of his wife (2.9) and friends in the Book of Job the Patient (see intro.) that Job blaspheme God. (*Integrity* in 27.5 is the same word, "tam," translated "blameless" in 1.1 and 2.3.) In so doing, of course, Job would have enabled the Adversary rather than God to win the wager described in 1.6–12; 2.2–8.

27.1–23: Job's speech continues. 2–6: Notwithstanding his loss of property, children, and health, and the friends' urging him to blaspheme God, he is swearing an oath by God not to blaspheme God. **2:** *By God*, i.e., "I swear." Having been urged by his wife to blaspheme God, Job refuses to do so (2.9–10). **4:** *My lips will speak no wrong*, the content of the oath referred to in v. 2. Consequently, each clause begins with "'im," which means "no, nor" in the context of an oath. Here we see the dramatization of what the narrator asserted in 2.10: "Job said nothing

—1538—

Figure 9. Contemporary study Bibles—here the Jewish Publication Society's *Jewish Study Bible*—inform readers about important historical critical discoveries. Here the editors mention common understandings of Chapter 27 as "a collection of leftovers" and 28 as "a separate composition" but suggest that "interpreting the book as a complete work" one can see them as Job's long-delayed response to questions unaddressed from the frame story. *Jewish Study Bible*, edited by Adele Berlin and Marc Zvi Brettler (New York: Oxford University Press, 2004), p. 1538. Photograph courtesy of the Jewish Publication Society and Oxford University Press.

the book.[7] To make things even more puzzling, its last lines,

> And he [God] said to humankind,
> "Truly, the fear of the Lord, that is wisdom;
>   and to depart from evil is understanding."
>   (28:28)

which so clearly echo the language of the prologue, appear to be an addition to an addition.

And yet, as we've seen, premodern interpreters have seen Chapter 28, and especially its mini-theophany, not only as an organic part of the text, but as the key to the book of Job and to the character of its protagonist. Its combination of poetic skill and levelheadedness suggests Job is aware of what he's saying elsewhere. Modern interpreters have prized it, too. One nineteenth-century Christian interpreter celebrated 28:28 as the "clasp" of the book.[8] Progressive rabbi and scholar Leo Baeck thought it the heart of the book of Job,[9] and the recent evangelical *Africa Bible Commentary* argues that it captures the "main theme of the book."[10] Scholars now often suggest that Chapter 28 is a sort of poetic meditation by the narrator of the book—assuming, of course, that the narrator isn't Job himself. If it is understood to be in Job's voice, either in the midst of his ordeal or as part of his self-narration, it can't but change the way in which his character is understood throughout.

The speeches of Elihu are the clearest insertions to the text. There is no mention of the impetuous young man in the prose *or* poetry before his sudden appearance. Job doesn't respond to his speeches. And after Elihu finishes speaking he is never heard from or mentioned again. When the prose resumes after the divine speeches, God announces himself wroth with Eliphaz and his *two* friends (42:7). Further, Elihu's is the only Hebrew name in the text. He is the only character to refer to the other characters by name, or to quote their words. Indeed, he *anticipates* words that have not yet been spoken—stealing thunder from the very mouth of God. To many readers, Elihu has seemed to add nothing but hot air. He seems a tedious intrusion and an irritating postponement of God's answer to Job. Elihu is routinely omitted from synopses of the text. Stephen Mitchell's widely used poetic translation omits both the Hymn to Wisdom and the entire Elihu section.

Even if he seems a redundancy, however, interpreters ancient and modern have insisted on Elihu's importance to the book as a whole. As we have seen, Maimonides argued that this very appearance of redundancy was the way scripture hid its most precious message from undiscerning viewers. Elihu is *supposed* to sound derivative. In fact he provided an interpretation of Job's suffering closer to what (according to the prose frame) was actually happening.

Job in Exile   205

The fact that Elihu is not mentioned in the divine judgment can be interpreted entirely differently. We're not told that he left the scene after his speeches. Why not conclude that he was there when God spoke and *not* condemned by him for speaking wrongly? Many Jewish commentators made this argument. Perhaps in response, Christian interpreters like Aquinas read the angry words opening the first divine speech—"Who is this that darkens counsel by words without knowledge?" (38:2)—as directed at Elihu! (Job is conveniently exonerated in the process.) Affection for Elihu is not restricted to premodern interpreters. One contemporary who sees the central argument of Job precisely in its poetry regards Elihu as the clearest representative of that view.[11] Another suggests we see Elihu as the first *reader* of the book of Job—a "dissatisfied reader" no less—inserting himself into the text as every successive reader will, too.[12] We may be like Elihu: our status as latecomers to Job's story is closer to Elihu's than to any of the other characters in the story.

Some interpreters have wondered if even the divine speeches are additions to an earlier text. After all, God comes barging in like a stranger. "It is as if He has belatedly stepped into a drama without having consulted the script," one has observed; "none of it: not even so much as the prologue."[13] Job's questions aren't even acknowledged, let alone answered.

And why two speeches instead of just one? Why make Job speak again, after he's said he would not speak again (40:5)? What do Behemoth and Leviathan add? But again, we must not suppose earlier interpreters had not considered these questions. For many, God's bypassing Job's questions was precisely the point. For Saadiah Gaon and Maimonides, it was the most important fact about the divine speeches that they did not touch the categories and questions of Job and his friends at all. The responses of Job to the two speeches also suggest that they had different functions. Stunned and cowed after the first, he seems resigned and accepting after the second—or is it the other way around? Some see Job satisfied by the first and actually joyful in the second. Much rests on how his final words (42:6), among the book's most obscure, are understood.

Historical critical method has been criticized for being fundamentally skeptical, but while it certainly can be, it can also be a good faith attempt to make sense of the Bible with the best tools modernity offers. It is too late to wish its discoveries away. The bounded world of scripture Kugel described has been exploded, just as the medieval cosmos of meaning was exploded by the discovery of infinite space. The quest for a certain and stable text can be understood as constructive, not destructive, a continuation of the Reformation's commitment to

scripture and not just the Enlightenment's commitment to move beyond it.

The historical critical understanding of the Bible
has not gone unchallenged, of course. Indeed, the
main reaction to it—inerrantist biblical literalism—is
the view taken by the majority of Bible users today.
This approach can be naïve, but most literalists take
"literal" less literally than their critics do, and are ca-
pable of vast erudition in their efforts to use only the
Bible to understand what the Bible is saying to them.
(See the *Ryrie Study Bible*, figure 10.) Literalism may
seem a return to the world of the "ancient interpreters" we explored in chapter 2, and it does indeed share
many of the four assumptions James Kugel describes.
In fact, "relevant" and "divinely granted" are a pretty
good account of their view. (Whether contemporary
forms of apologetics treat the Bible as "perfect" in
Kugel's sense is less clear.)

Biblical literalism does not, however, share the
foundational assumption that the Bible's meanings are "cryptic." This makes a huge difference. As
Kugel explains, the idea

that almost everything Scripture says is literally
true ... is one that would certainly have puzzled
the ancient interpreters. On the one hand, they
would have readily agreed that what the Bible reports did indeed happen ... On the other hand,

25"For ᵃwhat I fear comes upon me,
And what I dread befalls me.
26"I ᵃam not at ease, nor am I quiet,
And I am not at rest, but turmoil comes."

B **Eliphaz's First Speech,**
4:1–5:27

4 Then Eliphaz the Temanite
ᵃanswered,
2"If one ventures a word
with you, will you
become impatient?
But ᵃwho can refrain from
speaking?
3"Behold ᵃyou have
admonished many,
And you have strengthened
weak hands.
4"Your words have helped
the tottering to stand,
And you have strengthened
feeble knees.
5"But now it has come to
you, and you ᵃare
impatient;
It ᵇtouches you, and you
are dismayed.
6"Is not your ᵃfear of God
ᵇyour confidence,
And the integrity of your
ways your hope?
7"Remember now, ᵃwho
ever perished being
innocent?
Or where were the upright
destroyed?
8"According to what I have
seen, ᵃthose who plow
iniquity
And those who sow trouble
harvest it.
9"By ᵃthe breath of God
they perish,

And ᵇby the blast of His
anger they come to an
end.
10"The ᵃroaring of the lion
and the voice of the
fierce lion,
And the teeth of the young
lions are broken.
11"The ᵃlion perishes for lack
of prey,
And the ᵇwhelps of the
lioness are scattered.

12"Now a word ᵃwas
brought to me
stealthily,
And my ear received a
ᵇwhisper of it.
13"Amid disquieting
ᵃthoughts from the
visions of the night,
When deep sleep falls on
men,
14 Dread came upon me, and
trembling,
And made all my bones
shake.
15"Then a spirit passed by my
face;
The hair of my flesh
bristled up.
16"It stood still, but I could
not discern its
appearance;
A form was before my eyes;
There was silence, then I
heard a voice:
17 'Can ᵃmankind be just
before God?
Can a man be pure before
his ᵇMaker?
18 'ᵃHe puts no trust even in
His servants;
And against His angels He
charges error.
19 'How much more those
who dwell in ᵃhouses
of clay,

4:1 *Eliphaz.* The most sympathetic of Job's three friends, who speaks first and appeals to experience for authority. He was likely the eldest (15:10).
4:5 *it.* I.e., the calamity that had befallen Job.
4:7-9 Eliphaz declares that the wicked, not the innocent, perish. But this is not always true.
4:10-11 The meaning is this: Although wicked men may be strong, they cannot ultimately

prosper.
4:12-21 Eliphaz tried to bolster his argument by relating it to a vision he had had (vv. 15-16). He asks, "If angels cannot be considered trustworthy, how can man be?" (vv. 18-19). *before the moth.* I.e., sooner than the moth. *their tent-cord.* Death is likened to the collapse of a tent when the tent-cord is pulled up.

Figure 10. The Bible elucidates itself for Evangelical readers. On this page from the *Ryrie Study Bible* (New American Standard Version), Eliphaz's claim to have heard a figure in a dream ask "Can a man be pure before his Maker?" (4:17) is cross-referenced with Psalms, Proverbs, Ecclesiastes, Isaiah, Malachi, and Acts, as well as other lines from the Book of Job, spoken by Eliphaz, Bildad, Elihu, God, and Job himself. That God later reproves Eliphaz for not speaking rightly (42:7) is immaterial. Every word is from the same inspired source. Scripture taken from the NEW AMERICAN STANDARD BIBLE®, used by permission.

Job in Exile   209

they would also have dismissed such statements as obvious; Scripture's *important* message, they would say, is often hidden, so that only by going beyond the obvious can one arrive at its true meaning. It is precisely that message, they would tell fundamentalists, that you are missing.[14]

For the ancient interpreters the Bible didn't just bring the transcendent into our world, but showed us to be participants in a different order of causation and signification entirely. For all their suspicion of the "scientific" assumptions of historical critical work, biblical literalists share the modern world's understanding of a univocal reality. The Bible may be for them a talking book with numberless things to say to numberless people and situations, but it does this by a kind of metaphorical multiplication of local and fixed meanings.

In one way the findings of historical critical scholarship have forever changed the ways in which the Bible is read and lived. Whether we absorb its suggestions or confine ourselves to a received text for theological, traditional, or literary reasons, we are making a decision. These decisions are not made lightly, and are so shaped by communities of worship and interpretation that they may not feel like choices. But in a pluralistic age choice is inescapable, even if it is the choice to accept the tradition you were born into.[15] The challenge is to own the ways in which our choices of methods and interlocutors make biblical texts into books we can use. This need not be an occasion for mutual recrimination. It can be an opportunity for solidarity and learning.

Abiding with Job can be valuable here. Job too suffers the loss of a foundation for making sense of his world, and seeks resources in received wisdom, personal experience, the baffling processes of nature and God himself. Job's exchanges with his friends provide an object lesson in the difficulty of collective meaning-making. Yet as Maimonides suggested, the reactions of incompatible positions against each other might clear the way for deeper insight. The book of Job itself, like its protagonist, has undergone afflictions that undermine an easy certainty and resist the comforts of closure. Keeping patient company with it may be a way to glimpse truths beyond the types and shadows of modern understandings of the world and its meanings.

The Impatience of Job Interpreters

As awareness of the results of biblical scholarship has spread, a new story about Job seems to be on its way to becoming orthodoxy. On this view the book of Job is really two works, struggling in a death-match against each other. One is the prosaic and pious tale of a long-suffering and docile Job; the other is a poetic *cri de coeur* by a Job who is anything but docile. The former is often described as "Job the patient," recalling the tradition going back to James 5:11, the latter as "Job the impatient." Whether one thinks the prose was added to smother the poem, or, on the other hand, was torpedoed by it, the two stories are understood as fundamentally incompatible. Knowing them to be the work of different hands, readers are entitled to focus on one to the exclusion of the other. More, they are required to. The reader must take a side. Whichever story is taken to be true, the other is denounced as a calumny on Job's character. Many religious as well as secular interpreters urge us to vindicate the impatient Job.

Most such interpretations argue also that we should stand for and with Job against his friends—and often also against the God who torments him. Without quite admitting it, the champions of the impatient Job seek to become the *go'el*, the advocate who will inscribe Job's words in a book so that his memory will never be forgotten on the earth. Theirs is a stirring call to human solidarity in the face of complacency toward the suffering of others, and an object reminder that religious deference often silences the cries of the innocent. From the perspective of the text, however, the celebration of the impatience of Job is based on a simplification and leads to further simplifications. As we have just seen, the text is composed of many more than just two parts. Over its history, its several parts have moved in and out of the foreground of interpretations like the elements of a mobile. The supposedly forced choice between patience and impatience is really a legacy of the modern struggle between theodicy and ethics, a version of the call to people of conscience to free themselves of the blinders of traditional religion.

Reading the book of Job as either supporting or contesting religious dogmatism reproduces Enlightenment stereotypes of "dark ages" of hypocrisy and pusillanimity in thrall to a capricious and tyrannical God. The "patience" of the prologue's Job is seen as an emblem of downtrodden docility, a celebration of the unenlightened believer unable and unwilling to call God and tradition to account for the injustice and meaninglessness of human experience. Premodern interpreters are arraigned for allowing the prose frame Job to eclipse the truth-telling Job of the poem. Whether we believe that the wool was pulled over their eyes by the tradition of the "patient" Job, or that they were themselves incapable of seeing farther, their interpretations are thought to demonstrate the bad faith of the "ages of faith." Unwilling to raise their voices to demand an intelligible universe and a morally accountable God, they silenced those who dared to challenge their hollow pieties.[16]

This is of course a misrepresentation both of premodern interpretations of the book of Job and of the religious worlds these interpretations supposedly show. While the legend of the patient Job was a constant companion to the book of Job, at least some premodern readers saw the poetic portion as showing how a virtuous person grieves, and as showing the true heart of "patience" to be closer to protest than moderns imagine. Job's most rebellious words were often explained away as driven by physical pain and grief, but premodern readers did not simply ignore them. Closer experience of the agonies of sickness and loss may, indeed, have made them better listeners than moderns are, hearing the anguish and delirium of the flesh where we may just see a mind pushed to its limits. To them Job's protests are remarkable not for how far they go but for going no farther. If the words of the "Hymn to Wisdom" (Chapter 28) are spoken by Job, one can hear in them a hard-won insight of body as well as mind.

Knowing the "Hymn to Wisdom" to be an addition, however, can we still read its tempering of Job's voice this way, even if we wish to? Must we not see these words as forced, whether by accident or design, through the clenched teeth of a Job who decisively was not (at least at that stage) prepared to accept a divine monopoly on wisdom? The Job of the immediately succeeding chapters is as incandescent with protest as the Job who comes before it. Problematic as it may be, however, simply wishing the Hymn to Wisdom away is not an option, especially if we wish to be part of the conversation about Job of the past two millennia.

Some modern readers never get a chance to encounter the Hymn to Wisdom at all, whether as bug or as feature. Many readings of the book of Job pass over it in silence or omit it entirely. Others also drop the speeches of Elihu, downplay or even eliminate the frame story, or omit one or both of the divine speeches. René Girard's provocative reading of the book of Job as recounting an archetypal scapegoating scenario works with such a purified text.[17] The later additions conceal what is really going on. In his recent poetic adaptation David Rosenberg omits even the friends, giving us the monologue that many modern readings have implied that the book of Job essentially is. Rosenberg suggests that the speeches of the friends were added to an inspired rant whose true nature not only doesn't need them but is misrepresented as part of a dialogue. Job speaks out of the bitterness of his soul:

> O earth, cover not over my blood!
> don't be a tomb a museum
> for my miserable poem
>
> my cry against this sinking
> leave my voice uncovered
> a little scar on your face
>
> face of the earth
> open to the sky
> the universe
>
> where you can see
> a justice waiting to be discovered
> like an inner referee
>
> the deep seat of conscience
> where a creator sits
> handing me these words themselves[18]

Rosenberg cites a famous saying of John Coltrane to explain his choice of jazzy American language: "You got to keep talking / to be real" (394).

Read on its own, the "poem of Job" is a magnificent work, in many ways more universal than the specific story of a specific person. Gone are the embarrassments of Job's wealth and social prominence, along with the rote destruction of his life and the galling restoration. Job now speaks for anyone who suffers unjustly. Removing the prologue allows Job to be an everyman. He is no longer necessarily a moral paragon; it is sufficient that he be decent, a "serious man." He commends himself to us by the passion and honesty of his speech, not by the standards of law or God.

It must be asked, however, if the "poem of Job" can do its work without at least the memory of the prologue. Does the poem not rely on the well-known story of the patient Job to establish the character of Job, and of God? (We saw already in Baba Bathra that, were it not written in the text, we should not dare to imagine that God wagers with the satan.) Without the prologue, we don't know that Job is right and his friends wrong about his past virtue. With it, we have not only the narrator's but God's word that Job is "blameless and upright" (1:1, 1:8, 2:3). Something important is achieved also by letting readers know the real reason for Job's afflictions. They show that Job's questions about God's motives are entirely warranted. God himself will, in the epilogue, confirm that Job spoke "rightly" (42:7).

Whether we accept that God has his reasons or not, a mismatch between God's ways and man's efforts to understand them is put in place long before the theophany. In its way the prologue also closes off the possibility of a mere faith solution. It is not a mystery why Job suffers, though it is for all the people in the story. In all these ways the prologue doesn't undermine the "impatience" of Job at all, but grounds it.

The epilogue might seem harder to vindicate. The restoration of Job's goods—in double, no less— and Job's wordless acceptance have troubled many. Would not the story end better by not ending? In real-life disasters no restoration is possible. In particular, the suggestion that Job's dead children might be replaced like so many head of cattle—indeed, by more beautiful ones!—just seems obscene. The epilogue seems the worst kind of bad faith, allowing God to press reset after playing his cruel game. How can Job play along? Yet many interpreters have seen in Job's continued life the profoundest mystery and challenge of the text. The narrator of Kierkegaard's *Repetition* found the possibility of Job's living on to be the profoundest of insights into the mystery of living in time. Fyodor Dostoevsky's Zosima wonders how Job, remembering his lost children, could "be completely happy as before with the new ones, however dear they were to him?" then insists: "But he could, he could."[19]

The epilogue is widely regretted because it seems to prove the friends' retributionist view of God right after all. Fortune and misfortune *are* God's payment for good and bad behavior. Yet it's too simple to describe the framing prologue and epilogue as committed unproblematically to the retributionist view represented in the dialogues by the friends, while the poetic speeches of Job are something else entirely. The Job of the prologue accepts both evil and good as gifts of God (1:21, 2:10), while retributionist assumptions underlie much of what the poetic Job says. Indeed, the logic of retribution is the very framework for Job's protest. If God doesn't proportion fortune to virtue, what has Job to complain about? What is Job demanding of God if it is not that he be the kind of God retributionist theologies describe?[20]

Even if one could separate the "patient" and the "impatient" Job stories, one would end up impoverishing both. We have seen that the "patience" exemplified by Job is deepened if his grief and protest are understood as elements of it. The voice of the "impatient" Job, too, may ring most clearly from the book of Job taken as a whole, not just from the poetic speeches. This is not to say that Joban patience and impatience are ultimately the same—although the same text may inform both. The book of Job works as a polyphonic text, challenging any rendering that irons out its complexity. The text we inherit is sprung like a trap for pieties of every kind, including the piety of a principled impiety.

A Job on Every Road

There were more reasons for the appearance of the impatient Job than just those opened up by historical criticism of the Bible. At the center of contemporary western religious experience and reflection was the near destruction of God's chosen people in the Shoah. The silence of God at Auschwitz forced the theodicy question in terrible new ways, if less for most Christians than one might have hoped. In the twentieth century of the Common Era, at last, Job became Jewish, and Jewish questions about a God who hides his face became universal.

When Elie Wiesel, a man sometimes referred to as the "Job of Auschwitz," accepted the Nobel Peace Prize in 1986, he made Job the face of every oppressed person in history:

> Job, our ancestor. Job, our contemporary. His ordeal concerns all humanity. . . . He demonstrated that faith is essential to rebellion, and that hope is possible beyond despair. The source of his hope was memory, as it must be ours. Because I remember, I despair. Because I remember, I have the duty to reject despair.[21]

By this time Wiesel had kept company with Job for more than half a century, and found him a necessary companion in his struggles with cataclysm and silence. The relationship was not always amicable. It changed and deepened as history raged around them. In these changes we can get a glimpse of the overwhelming challenges posed by the encounter with catastrophe, the obligations of memory and the demands of survival, and the book of Job's significance for each.

Wiesel reports that as a child in Auschwitz he "had ceased to pray. How I sympathized with Job! I did not deny God's existence, but I doubted his absolute justice."[22] He witnessed a "trial of God" like the one for which Job hopes, conducted by Hasidic rabbis, and was astounded at the outcome. God was condemned, but prayers continued. In the communities of survivors, too, Job's "tale was in high style . . . every survivor of the holocaust could have written it."[23] Wiesel himself was lecturing on the book of Job to fellow survivors in France already in 1946. Job's protest spoke to the moment like no other biblical voice, but what was one to do with his ultimate submission to a blustering God? Like the protagonist of one of his first novels, Wiesel "never ceased resenting Job. That biblical rebel should never have given in."[24]

Wiesel has spent a career struggling with the necessity and impossibility of telling what happened to a disbelieving or indifferent world, a world that at first didn't want to know, and later claimed it already knew. A half century later Wiesel described his generation as one whose "tragedy and . . . memories are drowning in noise"[25] as scholars, psychologists, and artists make the Shoah their topic. Constantly returning to the book of Job, Wiesel's work has probed and tested the limits of language and silence, fiction and fact. Can the same language describe the world most of us live in and the parallel inverted world of the death camps? Can language do justice to unjust suffering of any kind?

In the introduction to an early collection of writings, Wiesel tells of meeting a rabbi who had known him and his grandfather before the catastrophe. On hearing that Wiesel wrote fiction the rabbi was indignant. He should write about truth! "Things are not that simple, Rebbe," Wiesel replied, "Some events do take place but are not true; others are—although they never occurred."[26] This paradox of history and truth structures Wiesel's relationship with the book of Job, a work he came to see as true fiction, fiction come true but a truth unthinkable except as fiction.

The closing chapter of Wiesel's *Messengers of God* of 1975 is devoted to Job and his book.[27] Originally entitled "Job, or revolutionary silence," the essay excavates Job's silences, and offers them as the culmination of Wiesel's account of the challenge of faith. The mysterious man from Uz was from everywhere

and nowhere, he begins, invoking the theories assembled in the Baba Bathra. Over the course of history, however, Job became Jewish. Wiesel evokes
the time after the war when Job "could be seen on
every road of Europe."[28] Baba Bathra's unnamed
sage who thought Job never lived, the one who inspired Maimonides to see the whole book as a parable, speaks again through Wiesel's understanding
of the powers and limits of fiction:

> There were those who claimed that Job did exist
> but that his sufferings are sheer literary inven-
> tion. Then there were those who declare that
> while Job never existed, he undeniably did suf-
> fer. (215)

Elements in Job's story have seemed merely fic-
tional, but their truth has been confirmed in history as Jews have lived them. As Jews "attempt to
tell our own story, we transmit his" (211–12). Wiesel
is thinking of the sufferings of Job, not yet of Job's
life after the restoration of his wealth and family.

Wiesel is enthralled by the Job of "passionate
rebellion," whose challenge is not met by God's
speeches. God's words are at the level of generali-
ties and concepts. Job's legitimate demand was for
an accounting of his particular experience, and especially of his suffering. This is why his submissive
response to God's speeches leaves Wiesel "deeply

troubled." "No sooner had God spoken than Job repented" (231). How can "our hero, our standard bearer," who so fearlessly protested against divine injustice, have "surrendered unconditionally" when he had done no wrong? (232).

So disappointed is Wiesel that he would "prefer to think that the Book's true ending was lost" (233). Perhaps it was excised as a condition for getting a place in the scriptures. He imagines an original ending to the story in which Job never repented, and never stopped challenging God. Instead of settling, he "succumbed to his grief an uncompromising and whole man" (233). Rather than becoming the "accomplice" of the killer of his children, this Job took his passionate protest with him to his grave. He would want us, too, to refuse God's inadequate answers to human questions (234). If Job is right to demand more of God, we are right to demand more of the disappointing Job of the received text.

But a Job who refuses to compromise may be there in the text after all. Resisting the historical crit-ical temptation, Wiesel instead turns the text in the manner of the midrashim. If something in the text troubles us, it is an opening, not a closing. It is an invitation to dig deeper. Surely the unseemly haste of Job's capitulation and the strange incongruity of his words are things we are *supposed* to notice and be disturbed by, not to accept at face value. Rightly

understood they surely show that Job merely "pre-
tends to abdicate" (234): "By repenting sins he did
not commit, by justifying a sorrow he did not deserve, he communicates to us that he did not believe
in his own confessions" (235). We should not, either.

Wiesel doesn't have to challenge its textual integrity to make the book of Job one he can live with.
He accounts for incongruities in the text by attend-
ing to the silences within and between Job's words.
Job does not disappoint after all. His reproach to
God continues in silence, the only form possible
in the face of misplaced demands for closure. The
story's happy end is rendered less objectionable
when read this way, too. We can imagine that the
joy of Job's second family does not displace but is
ever haunted by mourning and is attended by silent
protest to God over the loss of the first.

Wiesel has found a deep kinship between protest and a kind of silence, but the Nobel Prize address' problems of memory and hope are not yet
explicit concerns. Job's refusal to "move on" from
injustice and tragedy challenges us not to yield in
our demand for meaning and justice. Our lives may
go on, but we owe it to those whose lives were cut
short never to forget the injustices of the past, and
never to surrender to an apparently unjust God.
With time, however, Wiesel's Job becomes a figure
also of new life. The 1986 Nobel address shows not

only how rebellion can be part of faith, but how memory of the lost makes possible an affirmation of creation and an embrace of the future.

> Let us remember Job who, having lost everything—his children, his friends, his possessions, and even his argument with God—still found the strength to begin again, to rebuild his life. Job was determined not to repudiate the creation, however imperfect, that God had entrusted to him.[29]

The sense in which Job had "lost . . . his argument with God" is not explained, but it seems that the relationship with God has been restored. A new reading of the theophany is implied: creation is "imperfect." Also new is the suggestion that God has "entrusted" this imperfect world to human care.

Wiesel continues to lecture on Job, and continues to find new meaning in his book. An essay Wiesel published in 1998 argues that if Job isn't going to continue his questions, we should. His silent protest has revealed an understanding of paradox, the paradox of a rebellious faith. This form of faith was one that Job possessed even before God addressed him. "The drama of Job, the tragedy of Job as well as his troubling mystery" are all concentrated in 13:15, which can be read in two ways: "See, he will kill me; I have no hope," or "Though he slay me, yet will I trust in him." The former is the *ketiv*, the meaning as written, the latter the *qere*, the vocalized meaning—a significant fact in the context of Wiesel's reflections on the language of silence.[30] This understanding of 13:15's power and danger is not new to Wiesel (see figure 6). It gains a new importance now because Job's struggle with the false friends has taken on new salience.

After working for half a century to break the silence about Auschwitz, Wiesel now wonders if anyone has understood that only silence is ultimately adequate to the paradoxical task of remembering and hoping. A new interpretation of the sudden end of Job's speaking emerges. No longer a scandal to be explained in terms of lost originals or continuing subterranean protest, it is the demonstration of a wisdom like that of Qohelet.

> [Job] stopped protesting as soon as God spoke to him out of the whirlwind. There is a time for protest and a time for restraint, a time for memory and a time for forgiveness, a time for rebellion and a time for penitence.[31]

Job's silence seems no longer to be protesting the failures of God, but part of a deepened relationship with God.

Wiesel recalls a midrash that interprets God's questions to Job not as obfuscation or bravado but as something else entirely: God addressing Job as a teacher addresses a student.

> In so doing, God offers Job—and through him all of us—a new understanding of the mysterious man-God relationship: it is not defined by that which distinguished question from answer but by that which separates one question from another.[32]

It is in questioning, not in answers, that faith consists. The name of God—*El*—resides within the word for questioning, *she'elah*.[33] Job had "learned that he lived in a world that was cold and cynical—a world without true friends," but a world in which "God seeks to join man in his solitude."[34]

The book of Job has accompanied Wiesel through seven decades, and it is no surprise that he should have discovered new meanings in this inexhaustible text as the world changed around him. We can learn from his long engagement with it that the book of Job speaks differently to people in the midst of disaster, in its immediate aftermath, and in mourning its victims. It is heard differently when negotiating the impossible task of reintegrating into a world that will not acknowledge the disaster and when finding the strength to rebuild a community for the future without forgetting crippling loss. Through thick and thin, Wiesel has returned to the book of Job with all its rough edges and striven to speak rightly of it.

Wiesel's eloquent struggles with the paradoxes of fiction and truth, justice and memory and hope, were not the only theological responses to the Shoah. Some Jewish thinkers had no difficulty at all. As already in biblical times God's people had once again turned their back on him, and merited his chastisement. The extent of the punishment was commensurate to the crime of apostasy. But the history of the People of Israel, in biblical time and postbiblical, showed that God did not abandon his errant people. Such interpreters had no reason to turn to Job. Even the situation of those Jews who had died for the sins of others was not illuminated by the story of the stiff-necked man from Uz.

For others, the Shoah marked the point at which faith in God, any God, became unsustainable. Richard Rubenstein is the best known thinker for whom the Holocaust necessitated a fundamental rethinking of Judaism—without the idea of chosenness, and, perhaps, without God. Wiesel can appeal to the example of Job because he was one who somehow found his faith deepened in the cataclysm, writes Rubenstein, but those "who went to their death immediately" are more like Job's children."[35] Their death should remind us of the frequency of divine infanticide in the Bible. The track record of

Job in Exile   229

the God of the Jews is, in fact, too awful to contemplate. Rubenstein imagines that a modern-day comforter might counsel Job to admit to guilt, even though he was innocent. Lie, or the truth will out that God is a demon—if he exists at all.[36]

Job's experience of divine silence, followed by an encounter of divine presence and overwhelming speech, seems inadequate to Auschwitz. We have seen that some of the ancient interpreters thought Job's sojourn on the ash heap lasted years. Nevertheless, God's silence in Job is as nothing compared to the silence of God during the Shoah. André Néher has suggested that Job's persistence offers an image of a suspension bridge across divine silence, with God waiting on the other side. The Holocaust by contrast seems to represent a broken arch.[37] Could any bridge cross such a gulf of agony and death? The biblical record and, especially, the book of Job make that question finally unanswerable. But one thing is clear. If we stop asking, we will never be found by an answer. God himself may be dependent on our persistence in asking.

God in Exile

We have seen how Job's experience of confronting God on his own, without the support or mediation of a religious community or its rituals, spoke more to modern religious struggles than did frayed covenants or fractured churches. For a time the worlds of nature and human endeavor made sense on their own, and religious questions gravitated to exceptional experiences of evil and mystery like Job's. Eventually cosmos and history themselves came to seem senseless. Even before the catastrophe of the Shoah, modern artists and thinkers described a world of meaningless human striving and suffering, at best haunted by the memory of a God who had died.

Yet Job was still standing. Our final interpretation of the book of Job, German Jewish philosopher and essayist Margarete Susman's *Job and the Destiny of the Jewish People*, was written in exile in Switzerland during World War II. As war and genocide raged around her, Susman found that only this biblical book could made sense of the unthinkable catastrophe. How could a godly and innocent people be so hated, so afflicted? Susman proposed a radical realignment of Jewish existence with Job's experience off the map of the history of covenants. The book of Job was the book of destiny and prophecy—the *Schicksalsbuch*—of the Jewish people, and so of all humanity.[38]

Job and the Destiny of the Jewish People engages all the parts of the book of Job that have been important in the history of its interpretation, with the interesting exception of Elihu's speeches. Susman's

Job was a man of consummate virtue and piety. He had been so generous to others that they came to rely on him like the rain. Uniquely aware of human nothingness before God, he performed sacrifices for others and even for sins committed unawares or only in thought. Such scruple became a temptation to God, one of whose sons—Satan—was given permission to do everything but take Job's life. Job, knowing the source of his sufferings to be God, wished never to have been born to this painful, perplexing relationship. Friends found him so deformed by his suffering that they could not at first recognize him. Others who had benefited from Job's charity before turned away from him and reviled him.

> If even one of them had cried out, "Why you? Why not me?" they would have needed none of the profundity of their speeches, but would have experienced something of his own afflictedness. But they speak from the outside, objectively, generally. (63)

This failure of human friendship pushed Job closer to the very source of his pain, and so he was able to find in himself hope for a messiah. In his struggle with God. he never doubted God's existence but only demanded to know what God wanted of him (179).

Eventually God appeared to Job as Creator, revealing nature to be his work, and Job understood and embraced his role as a creation. Job learned nothing new here. The Hymn to Wisdom, for instance, made clear that he understood that only God knew where wisdom was (188). Yet hearing it from God himself changed everything. In addressing him God acknowledged Job's individuality, something even Job had lost the capacity to do. Job never asked for the restoration of his life, and could even imagine it only once he had come to see all of creation as miracle, rather than the work of justice (199).

This reading of the book of Job enabled Susman to understand the Holocaust, precisely in its irrational and unprecedented horror, as a sign of continued divine commitment to Israel. Job's virtue and near-obsessive piety corresponded to the Jewish religious commitment to serve and suffer for the nations. Susman recalls a midrash that every other people refused the Law, as accepting it entailed suffering for the sins of all; only the Jews accepted it. The experience of evile made erst while beneficiaries—Christians, whose savior was a Jew—turn against the Jews, the scapegoat described already in Isaiah (213). Later friends, too, proved unable to comprehend Israel's special destiny. They refused to acknowledge its innocent suffering as an emblem of the true nature of all human existence. When what had seemed the closest friendship— the German Jewish synthesis—turned murderous,

Jews could find only in God, whom they knew to be their ultimate persecutor, an acknowledgment of their experience.

This was a terrible discovery, not a comforting one. God's commitment to Israel permitted the nations to wreak havoc with it. The most unsettling teaching of the book of Job, Susman argued, was that Satan was a "son of God." This suggested that even Hitler may have had a necessary part to play in unfolding the messianic story (214). Yet God also would not let Israel die—even when it wished to. Susman commended the early Zionists, but warned against the wish to be a nation like other nations. Theodor Herzl's hope was Satan's last trap (213), the correlate of Job's wish never to have been born (188).[39] Reminding her readers that David was not permitted to build a temple, Susman wrests Jewish destiny from the Davidic covenant, anchoring it instead in the Joban *Schicksalsbuch*.

The Jewish people, Susman wrote,

> has no existence for itself. As representative of all the earth's oppressed and insulted it is like Job separated out to represent human existence itself, for the ever new posing of the final human questions. (234)

And yet it was also "a glorious thing to be a Jew, for it means being human" (154). Making its life in diaspora, Israel alone lives a truly human existence, aware that its true source lies beyond territory and world history. It lives and must live "in pure space, in pure time, remaining still in pure creation, more alive, farther from death, closer to humanity than the other peoples" (112). Jewish witness to truly human existence has never been more important than in the modern age, a time in which the human as well as the divine have become "illegible" (171).

Jewish existence proleptically represents the peace and brotherhood of the end of time. Yet Jewish history illuminated by the story of Job shows that Israel will receive no thanks for this from the nations, but rather curses. The nations deny their createdness. Their attempts to be *sui generis* in fantasies of blood and soil lead inevitably to war. In ways laid out in Isaiah's account of the suffering servant, God permits the nations satanically to project their own demons on defenseless Israel. In this innocent suffering, however, Israel is able to discover and maintain the messianic hope that human existence might be more than hatred, misery, and war. It is no wonder that modern Jewish thinkers like Marx and Cohen, Bergson and Simmel, Freud and Rosenzweig were the first to sense the hollowness of modern humanism, Susman asserts, and the need for messianic hope.

Susman begins and ends her book with quotations from a modern Jewish writer whose entire *oeuvre* has been interpreted as a commentary on the book of Job even though Job is never mentioned: Franz Kafka. She was one of the first to link Kafka's evocations of the mute fruitlessness of modern experience to the social, cognitive, and spiritual crises of Job. A line from Kafka's diary (January 10, 1920) limns Susman's closing account of that messianic hope which, paradoxically, can arise only from the most total devastation:

> It is no refutation of the premonition of a final rescue when the imprisonment is unchanged the following day or even more severe, or even when it is expressly explained that it will never end. For all of that can be the necessary precondition for the final rescue. (238)

Kafka is not an obvious apostle of hope, but Susman's conception of hope is not the usual one. Kafka's rigorous evocations of dehumanization are the most powerful accounts of what true hope and true humanity might be, precisely through their absence. "Metamorphosis," the tale of a man who awakes to find himself transformed into a monstrous insect, describes modern Jewish, and through it, all modern human experience. Its protagonist Gregor Samsa is not only "a Job . . . ejected entirely from human community" but so estranged from his own humanity that he "cannot present his

fate to God and demand to be dealt with in a human way" (152).

Susman first laid out the analogy of Job and Jewish experience in a 1929 essay on Kafka, years before
the cataclysm.[40] Like Job the Jews know what only
the truly innocent sufferer can know—that individual innocence does not register in the relationship of
humanity and God, a relationship defined rather by
a general human guilt. Modern Jews, Susman argues,
are triply homeless. They are exiled from a homeland,
from nature. In refusing to convert to Christianity,
they are exiled from history. And the disenchanted
modern European civilization to which they have
assimilated has itself lost sight of the divine, and of
the human. The Christian (or ex-Christian) still has
the world and history, for his God once appeared
in it. The Jew has nothing but a transcendent God
beyond nature and culture, whom she cannot help
constantly seeking and addressing. She is Job.

The awful truth is that the only way to encounter
God unambiguously is in a suffering that defies nature and history as well as justice, and, thus, alone,
can be known to be a divine sign. This is what Kafka
and his characters seek. There is no lament in Kafka,
only a tireless seeking for the law that might explain
and redeem existence, restore humanity. "Herein
lies what is so strange, so profoundly religiously shat-
tering about Kafka's God-remote world," Susman

wrote: "it is seen not from the world, from life, but from God, measured against him and judged by him." Everything is in "indecipherable and uncanny relation" in the world of Kafka's writing, and we "never know which link in the endless chain we are touching." What has been described as Kafka's "perceptual nightmare" may seem the end of the road for the human project to discern a "depth dimension" to our experience.[41] Yet Susman finds a messianic hope in the way Kafka's world, so ruthlessly rendered in its "God-remoteness," nevertheless calls for the affirmation of every part of it as, perhaps, the "necessary precondition for final salvation."

Margarete Susman's argument that the book of Job, more than the covenant of David, describes Jewish history and destiny makes Job's place off the map of history decisive. Job had been a sideshow to the story of Israel, just as the story of the Jews in diaspora had been for the centuries of Christian history. Now that the idols of nation, nature, and history are crumbling, God and human destiny have become legible again—though only in negative, and in the most anguished forms of affliction and marginalization. The lesson is a hard one, bitterly hard. But if we recognize Job and Kafka as prophets, there is still hope for human life.

Our time in western history has been described as a "secular age," an era in which "naïve" religious faith is no longer possible. Even the most devoted believer in a faith is aware that many others do not share it.[42] Religious communities flourish, to the consternation of secularization theorists, but know the world is not theirs alone—or perhaps theirs at all. The shared default experience is of a neutral world of indifferent natural laws shared by cultures and communities projecting fragile meanings on or beyond it. Every human tradition may be a sideshow.

Job is the modern soul's guide as it navigates the religious experience of being off the map. He has offered a template for experiences of individual hopelessness since the books of Hours. His relationship with God, based on personal integrity in the absence of communal or covenantal support, resonates with modern disenchantment with religious institutions. And his book records the strange and painful discovery that God's presence is felt most keenly in what might otherwise seem his absences: in the ethical irrationality of the world, and especially in those experiences of loss and suffering that defy human conceptions of justice or meaning. God may be understood to be the instigator of innocent suffering or to be suffering alongside the innocent—or both. The book of Job is the Schicksalsbuch for all whose God is exiled from what was once his creation.

Conclusion

We have seen the book of Job studied, prayed, and performed. We have seen Job's story supplemented, his words turned, and even turned inside-out. He has been a gentile, a Jew, a fable, a task. He has been tested and judged, as has his God. Both may have grown in the encounter. His story has been that of the exceptional friend of God, of the proud, the humble, the virtuous, and finally of every person suffering inhuman ordeals. His travails have been thought to show the justice of God and its opposite, a learning, an unlearning, a capitulation, a protest. From the periphery of a covenantal tradition he has become the emblem of a decentered world.

At every turn, Job's story and his voice empowered and resisted readings, often at the same time. The book of Job would never allow itself to be fit into a larger interpretive claim for long; eventually some part of it always pushed against the proffered reading. Tensions and complexities that didn't fit a retelling would reappear, displaced, elsewhere. Lines and roles would shift around, but persist in their integrity. Some of these tensions are the results of what we now believe to be multiple authorship. Others trace from the lively countertraditions of the legend of Job that have danced alongside the biblical text for most of its history. Deeper tensions come from the profound questions Job's story raises, questions that challenge our sense of the meaning and justice of existence, the capacities of human goodness and understanding, the limits of language in dialogue, in monologue, and even in silence. The most painful depths of human experience may demand a text where figure and ground keep shifting.

In every case, readers and users struggle to make a *book* of Job, to articulate his story's meaning, and that of a world in which such stories can have meaning. It's tempting to try to be the *goʾel*—the redeemer, advocate, or vindicator—Job calls for, after wishing his words would be "inscribed in a book." The Jobs of our world, living and dead, need advocacy. But premodern interpretation of the book of Job suggests we shouldn't be so quick to condemn the friends—or to think we can do better than they.

We should strive to be better friends, not, as they did, to assume a God's-eye view:

> Have pity on me, have pity on me, O you my
> friends,
> for the hand of God has touched me!
> Why do you, like God, pursue me,
> never satisfied with my flesh? (Job 19:21–22)

Keeping company with Job, as friend or interpreter, is a worthy activity. Only the one who sees no challenge in Job or the questions his book is thought to raise should be dismissed. Recognizing that Job's questions are not only "unfinalized" in the book of Job but "unfinalizable,"[1] we may conclude only that our obligation is to keep the retelling going in all its difficulty. This means learning to listen to every part of the text, and perhaps also to every serious past attempt to enter the argument— joining the long line of interventions that began with Elihu. Showing why and how this might be done has been the intention of this book.

As we try to do right by a world of innocent suffering, suspended covenants, strained friendships, and a natural world marvelously oblivious to us and our values, the book of Job with its entourage of serious and creative interpreters will continue to be invaluable. Whatever heartbreaks or outrages arise, Job has been there—or his interpreters have—silent, shouting, or stammering. In a remarkable image of Job's placeless universality, poet Nelly Sachs likened him to the compass-like direction markers (originally marking the winds, gentle and stormy) on the margins of old maps: Job is the "wind rose of torments" on the map of human experience.[2]

It would be foolish to predict between what covers Job's story will find itself bound in the future, but contemporary trends make clear that its history is nowhere near ending. In the West, the book of Job has established itself as a work independent of the rest of the Bible. In university Great Books curricula it represents the monotheism now in exile in our secular age, a monotheism that demonstrates its universal value by stepping outside of its own salvation history. The book of Job converses eruditely with Sophocles, Nietzsche, and the Bhagavad Gita. In the broader culture it names the nagging sense of a dramatic dimension lost to modern life (think of the Joban film *A Serious Man*) as well as the presentiment that humanity, an insignificantly small part of the universe, may yet beat with its heart, especially in its sufferings and in efforts at goodness (think of the Joban film *The Tree of Life*).[3] In the world disclosed by science, we are finding that the blast of divine nature poetry might in fact be not only persuasive but consoling. Job speaks to the remnants of the covenantal monotheisms, and to

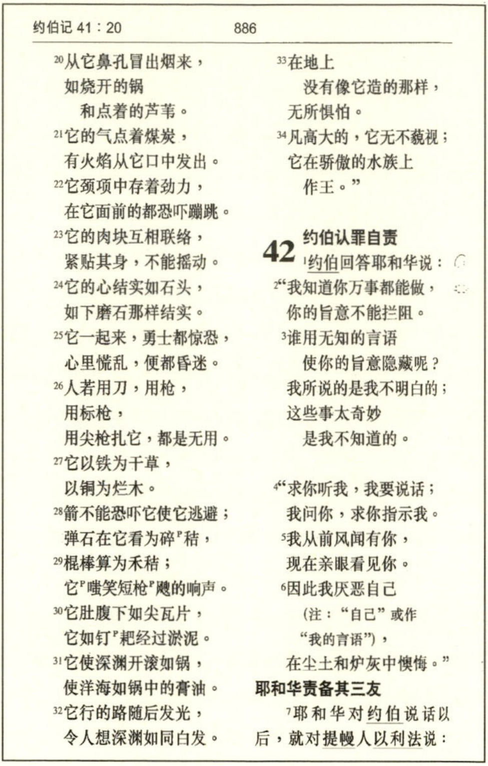
约伯记 41：20　　886

[20]从它鼻孔冒出烟来，
如烧开的锅
和点着的芦苇。
[21]它的气点着煤炭，
有火焰从它口中发出。
[22]它颈项中存着劲力，
在它面前的都恐吓蹦跳。
[23]它的肉块互相联络，
紧贴其身，不能摇动。
[24]它的心结实如石头，
如下磨石那样结实。
[25]它一起来，勇士都惊恐，
心里慌乱，便都昏迷。
[26]人若用刀，用枪，
用标枪，
用尖枪扎它，都是无用。
[27]它以铁为干草，
以铜为烂木。
[28]箭不能恐吓它使它逃避；
弹石在它看为碎[P]秸，
[29]棍棒算为禾秸；
它[P]嗤笑短枪[P]飕的响声。
[30]它肚腹下如尖瓦片，
它如钉[P]耙经过淤泥。
[31]它使深渊开滚如锅，
使洋海如锅中的膏油。
[32]它行的路随后发光，
令人想深渊如同白发。
[33]在地上
没有像它造的那样，
无所惧怕。
[34]凡高大的，它无不藐视；
它在骄傲的水族上
作王。”

42 **约伯认罪自责**

[1]约伯回答耶和华说：
[2]“我知道你万事都能做，
你的旨意不能拦阻。
[3]谁用无知的言语
使你的旨意隐藏呢？
我所说的是我不明白的；
这些事太奇妙
是我不知道的。

[4]“求你听我，我要说话；
我问你，求你指示我。
[5]我从前风闻有你，
现在亲眼看见你。
[6]因此我厌恶自己
（注：“自己”或作
“我的言语”），
在尘土和炉灰中懊悔。”

耶和华责备其三友

[7]耶和华对约伯说话以
后，就对提幔人以利法说：

Figure 11. With the aggressive campaigns to translate the (Christian) Bible into every known language, the book of Job now sounds in thousands of languages. In this 2012 Chinese version, Job's final words at 42:2–6 have been marked as a separate prayer. A note to 42:6 suggests that it may not be himself that Job "abhors" but only his words. Extracted from *Holy Bible—Union Version (Prayer and Promise Edition) Standard Size Large Print*, p. 886, reproduced by courtesy of The Chinese Bible International Limited, Hong Kong.

atheists, too. Kept alive by sufferers and seekers, Job may outlive his God.

In other parts of the world, Job's is not an old voice but a new one. Christian missionaries favor Job as particularly appealing to animists. Job's theo-centric words at 1:21 ("The Lord gave, and the Lord has taken away; blessed be the name of the Lord") remain his most widely known and quoted, but we should not assume they are always quietist. In the Congo they have challenged views of premature death as always the work of sorcery.[4] Read with African Evangelical eyes, the frame story's alternation between scenes of heaven and earth, which those in-fluenced by the "European Enlightenment" would rather discard, confirms that "what happens in the everyday world around us may reflect far greater con-flicts in the spiritual world."[5] Other readers are given speech by other parts of Job. Stigmatized South Afri-cans with HIV/AIDS have found in Job 3 a response to glib church uses of 1:21—biblical validation of their anguished wish never to have been born.[6] The book of Job offers powerful resources for respond-ing to HIV/AIDS outside a context of blame.[7] Job's capitulation can be seen as a lesson about situations where discourses of reason and justice are "still pow-erless" to challenge discourses of revelation.[8]

New readers have found in the book of Job both some of the Bible's most moving descriptions of

oppression and some of its most disdainful representations of the poor. Reading Job with his impov-
erished community in Lima, Peruvian liberation
theologian Gustavo Gutiérrez found it a primer
in how to speak of God from the heart of poverty
and communal oppression.[9] Job's discovery of the
suffering of the poor shows the way to a faith har-
monizing prophetic action with contemplation of
divine grace. Others have suggested that the story

Figure 12. (*facing page*) Jamaican artist Anna Ruth Henriquez
draws on family tradition—Jewish and Christian, European, African, Chinese, Indian, and Creole—in *The Book
of Mechtilde*, an illuminated book chronicling her mother's
life and slow death to cancer. The text of the book of Job (in
the American Standard Version) frames each scene. Here
Job's protestation of his innocence (Chapter 29) surrounds
an image of a daughter facing her mother's dying. Copyright
© Anna Ruth Henriques, 1997, *The Book of Mechtilde*, published by Alfred A. Knopf, Inc. The Jewish Museum, New
York. Purchase: The Reed Foundation Fund, The Fine Arts
Acquisition Committee Fund, and the United Congregation
of Israelites—Jewish Community of Jamaica, West Indies,
1999–84.29. Photo by Richard Goodbody, Inc. Photo credit:
The Jewish Museum, New York / Art Resource, NY.

of Job, "the greatest man of the east," can only have been written by and for the wealthy. The ubiquitous encomia to the text's sublimity and difficulty reveal it to be an ideological work that channels questions about the cause and meaning of oppression and inequality away from the political realm.[10] Elsa Tamez worries that Job will forget his fellow sufferers once his privilege is restored.[11]

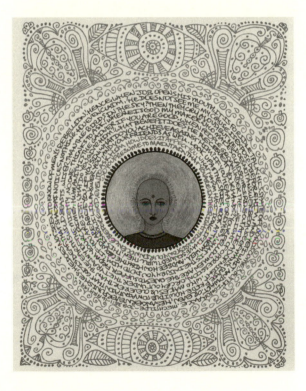

Each part of the book of Job has proved itself a resource and a challenge, a comfort and a provocation to deeper insight into the human and the divine. It waits for us when experience pushes thought and language to their breaking point. The book of Job continues to offer a voice for those confronting loss and pain in the midst of life, as well as for the pariah, the scapegoat, and the heretic. It shows the difficulty, perhaps even the impossibility, of speaking rightly of and to the Jobs in our midst. It is a call to self-vigilance and attention to the experiences of others, even when they call our fondest beliefs into question.

In its jarring polyphony and in its silences, the book of Job speaks to and for the broken. In its protagonist's persistence, it speaks of hope even in the depths of despair. In its unfinalizability, it offers a shared project for sufferers and witnesses, and an outline of a community of care. As we continue the work of binding shattered lives and worlds into livable wholes, we will continue also to make books of Job.

Introduction

1. 42:5-6. Very different renderings of the last verse are possible, ranging from the ravished to the resigned. Unless otherwise indicated, biblical translations are taken from the New Revised Standard Version. The work of an ecumenical team of translators, this is the preferred version of scholars.

2. D.J.A. Clines, "Why Is There a Book of Job and What Does It Do to You If You Read It?" in *The Book of Job*, ed. W.A.M. Beuken (Louvain: Peeters, 1994), 1-20.

3. For reasons only of convenience I will use the term "canonical" as shorthand for the authorized text of the book of Job shared by Jews and Western Christians, whose uses and interpretations are the main subject of this book.

4. Trans. Claude E. Cox in *A New Translation of the Septuagint*, ed. Albert Pietersma and Benjamin G. Wright (New York and Oxford: Oxford University Press, 2007), 671.

5. *New Translation of the Septuagint*, 696.

6. David J. A. Clines, *Job 21–37* (Word Biblical Commentary, vol. 18A) (Nashville: Thomas Nelson, 2006), 889.

7. Robert Eisen, *The Book of Job in Medieval Jewish Philosophy* (New York and Oxford: Oxford University Press, 2004).

8. Tewoldemedhin Habtu, "Introduction to the Wisdom Literature," in *Africa Bible Commentary*, ed. Tokuboh Adeyemo (Grand Rapids, MI: Zondervan, 2006), 569–70: 569.

9. Carol A. Newsom, *The Book of Job: A Contest of Moral Imaginations* (New York and Oxford: Oxford University Press, 2003), 16.

10. Robert Lowth, *Lectures on the Sacred Poetry of the Hebrews*, trans. G. Gregory, 2 vols. (London: J. Johnson, 1787; repr. London: Routledge/Thoemmes Press, 1995), 2:354.

11. Bruce Zuckerman, *Job the Silent: A Study in Historical Counterpoint* (New York: Oxford University Press, 1998).

12. Lawrence L. Besserman, *The Legend of Job in the Middle Ages* (Cambridge, MA: Harvard University Press, 1979).

13. Elsa Tamez, *The Scandalous Message of James: Faith Without Works Is Dead* (New York: Crossroad Publishing, 2002).

14. Judith R. Baskin, *Pharaoh's Counselors: Job, Jethro, and Balaam in Rabbinic and Patristic Tradition* (Chico, CA: Scholars Press, 1983).

15. See "The Poem of the Righteous Sufferer *Ludlul bêl nêmeqi*" and "The Babylonian *Theodicy*" in

W. G. Lambert, *Babylonian Wisdom Literature* (Oxford: Clarendon Press, 1960).

16. Newsom, *Book of Job*, 12.

17. Søren Kierkegaard, *Fear and Trembling, Repetition*, trans. Howard V. Hong and Edna H. Hong (Princeton: Princeton University Press, 1983), 204–5.

18. *Vaticanus Graecus* 29v; in Paul Huber, *Hiob: Dulder oder Rebell? Byzantinische Miniaturen zum Buch Hiob in Patmos, Rom, Venedig, Sinai, Jerusalem und Athos* (Düsseldorf: Patmos, 2006), 112.

19. Gregory the Great, *Morals in Job*, Epistle to Leander V, translations from *A Library of Fathers of the Catholic Church anterior to the Division of the East and West*, vols. 18–20 (Oxford and London: John Henry Parker and Rivington, 1844), much of it available at http://www.lectionarycentral.com /GregoryMoraliaIndex.html.

20. Elie Wiesel, *Messengers of God: Biblical Portraits and Legends*, trans. Marion Wiesel (New York: Random House, 1996), 215.

CHAPTER 1

Job in the Ancient Interpreters

1. Timothy Beal, *The Rise and Fall of the Bible: The Unexpected History of an Accidental Book* (New York: Houghton Mifflin Harcourt, 2011).

2. See Jack Miles, *God: A Biography* (New York: Vintage, 1996), 329f., and André Néher, *The Exile of the Word: From the Silence of the Bible to the Silence of Auschwitz*, trans. David Maisel (Philadelphia: JPSA, 1981).

3. Expos. interlin. Job 1. *Patrologia Latina* 23,1475C.

4. See Huber, *Hiob: Dulder oder Rebell?* and Stella Papadaki-Oekland, *Byzantine illuminated manuscripts of the Book of Job: A preliminary study of the miniature illustrations, its origin and development* (Turnhout, Belgium: Brepols, 2009).

5. Barbara Nelson Sargent-Baur, *Brothers of Dragons: "Job Dolens" and François Villon* (New York: Garland, 1990), 20.

6. *Biblia Pauperum*, 138.

7. References are to the translation by R. Thornhill in *The Apocryphal Old Testament*, ed. H.F.D. Sparks (Oxford: Clarendon Press, 1984), 617–48. For reasons of clarity I will refer to its protagonist as Jobab, although this translation does not.

8. Robert Frost, *A Masque of Reason* (New York: Henry Holt, 1945), 4.

9. Louis Ginzberg, *The Legends of the Jews*, trans. Henrietta Szold, 6 vols. (Philadelphia: JPSA, 1969), II:235.

10. James L. Kugel, *The Idea of Biblical Poetry: Parallelism and Its History* (New Haven, CT: Yale University Press, 1981), 103.

11. James L. Kugel, *How to Read the Bible: A Guide to Scripture, Then and Now* (New York: Free Press, 2007), 14–15.

12. Avivah Gottlieb Zornberg, *The Beginning of Desire: Reflections on Genesis* (New York: Schocken, 1995), 258, referencing *Genesis Rabbah. Bereshit Rabbah* 84:1 cites Job 9:23 and 3:26.

13. *Genesis Rabbah* 22:1. In *Tanh.* B: *Lev.* 9 and *Tanh.* B: *Num.* 157, Obadiah is also listed. See Baskin, *Pharaoh's Counselors*, 14, 133n28.

14. *Deuteronomy Rabbah* 2:3.

15. *Pesitqa Rabbati* 47, quoted in Baskin, *Pharaoh's Counselors*, 105.

16. *Exodus Rabbah*, 21:7; cp. *Genesis Rabbah* 57:4 and *j. Sota* 20d. See Baskin, *Pharaoh's Counselors*, 103, 242n15.

17. Baba Bathra, trans. Maurice Simon and Israel W. Slotki, in *The Babylonian Talmud: Seder Nezekin*, ed. Rabbi Dr. I. Epstein, 4 vols. (London: Soncino, 1961), vol. 2.

18. Maimonides, *Guide of the Perplexed* III.22, trans. Shlomo Pines, 2 vols. (Chicago: University of Chicago Press, 1963), 486–87.

19. *Midrash Rabbah—Leviticus*, trans. J. Israelstam and Judah J. Slotki (London: Soncino Press, 1983), 55. Job's friends' final words probably refer to Job 34:37.

20. Augustine, *City of God* XVIII.46.

21. Gregory the Great, *Morals in Job*, Epistle to Leander V, translations from *A Library of Fathers of the Catholic Church anterior to the Division of the East and West*, vols. 18–20 (Oxford and London: John Henry Parker and Rivington, 1844), much of it available at http://www.lectionarycentral.com/GregoryMoraliaIndex.html.

22. E.g., 4.32.65 but mainly book 33; see Susan E. Schreiner, *Where Shall Wisdom Be Found? Calvin's Exegesis of Job from Medieval and Modern Perspectives* (Chicago and London: University of Chicago Press, 1994), 40–41.

23. Schreiner, *Where Shall Wisdom Be Found?* 30–31.

24. Eleonore Stump, "Aquinas on the Sufferings of Job," in *Reasoned Faith: Essays in Philosophical*

Theology in Honor of Norman Kretzmann, ed.
Eleonore Stump (Ithaca and London: Cornell
University Press, 1993), 328–57, 345.

25. Schreiner, *Where Shall Wisdom Be Found?* 36.

CHAPTER 2

Job in Disputation

1. David Hume, *Dialogues Concerning Natural
Religion*, ed. Richard H. Popkin (Indianapolis and
Cambridge: Hackett, 1980), 63.

2. Marilyn McCord Adams and Robert Merrihew
Adams, *The Problem of Evil* (Oxford: Oxford University Press, 1990), 2–3.

3. Boethius, *The Theological Tractates; The Consolation of Philosophy* (London: Heinemann/Cam-
bridge, MA: Harvard University Press, 1918), 153.

4. Marilyn McCord Adams, *Horrendous Evils and
the Goodness of God* (Ithaca and London: Cornell
University Press, 2000), 7.

5. As we will see in connection with Maimonides'
thought, Islamic traditions engaged many of
the same debates. They are not discussed here
because the Q'uran's Job (Ayyub) differs widely
from the text shared by Jews and Christians. See
A. H. Johns, "Narrative, Intertext and Allusion
in the Qur'anic Presentation of Job," excerpted in
David B. Burrell, *Deconstructing Theodicy: Why
Job Has Nothing to Say to the Puzzle of Suffering*
(Grand Rapids, MI: Brazos, 2008), 51–82.

6. Maimonides, *Guide of the Perplexed* III.22, trans.
Shlomo Pines, 2 vols. (Chicago: University of
Chicago Press, 1963).

7. The manuscript, copied in 1602, is at the Jewish Theological Seminary in New York; see Eisen, *The Book of Job in Medieval Jewish Philosophy*, 246n82. For Saadiah's Job, see *The Book of Theodicy: Translation and Commentary of the Book of Job by Saadiah Ben Joseph Al-Fayyûmî*, trans. from the Arabic by L. E. Goodman (New Haven and London: Yale University Press, 1988); Eisen, *Book of Job in Medieval Jewish Philosophy*, 17–42; Burrell, *Deconstructing Theodicy*, 84ff.

8. Eisen, *Book of Job in Medieval Jewish Philosophy*, 222.

9. References are to Thomas Aquinas, *The Literal Exposition on Job, A Scriptural Commentary Concerning Providence*, trans. Anthony Damico (Atlanta, GA: Scholars Press, 1989).

10. Thomas Aquinas, *Summa Theologica*, Ia., Q. 2, A. 3, Obj. 1.

11. Thomas Aquinas, *Summa Contra Gentiles*, 3.71.10.

12. *Summa Theologica*, Ia.IIae, Q. 37, A. 2, ad 2.

13. *Summa Theologica*, Ia., Q. 13.

14. John Yocum, "Aquinas' Literal Exposition on Job," in *Aquinas on Scripture: An Introduction to his Biblical Commentaries*, ed. Thomas G. Weinandy, OFM, Daniel A. Keating, and John P. Yocum (London and New York: T. & T. Clark, 2005), 21–42, 22.

15. John Calvin, *Sermons on Job*, English translation of 1574 (facsimile edition Edinburgh and Carlisle, PA: Banner of Truth, 1993); sermon 71 (on Job 19:17), 335b.

16. Schreiner, *Where Shall Wisdom Be Found?* 120.

17. *Institutes of the Christian Religion*, trans. Henry Beveridge (Grand Rapids, MI: Eerdmans, 1989), 2:61. See also 3.17.1.

18. Sermon 1, *Sermons on Job*, 1b.

19. Ibid.

20. David C. Steinmetz, "Calvin as an Interpreter of the Bible," in *Calvin and the Bible*, ed. Donald K. McKim (Cambridge and New York: Cambridge University Press, 2006), 282–91, 290.

21. Sermon 147 (on Job 38:1–4), *Sermons on Job*, 689a. Cp. *Institutes* 1.13.1.

22. Martin Luther made the same point in his preface to the book of Job: "his words show what kind of ideas a man, however holy he may be, has against God, when he gets the notion that God is not God, but only a judge and wrathful tyrant." See *Prefaces to the Books of the Bible*, trans. C. M. Jacobs, in *Works of Martin Luther*, vol. VI (Philadelphia: A. J. Holman and The Castle Press, 1932), 383.

23. Sermon 110 (on Job 30:11–21), *Sermons on Job*, 514a.

24. Sermon 70 (on Job 19:13...), *Sermons on Job*, 328a.

25. Sermon 147 (on Job 38:1–4), *Sermons on Job*, 690b.

26. Sermon 71 (on Job 19:17), *Sermons on Job*, 333a.

27. Schreiner, *Where Shall Wisdom Be Found?* 132–33.

28. Susan E. Schreiner, "Calvin as an Interpreter of Job," in *Calvin and the Bible*, ed. McKim, 53–84, 58.

29. Sermon 129 (34:4–10), *Sermons on Job*, 610b.

30. Max Weber, "The Social Psychology of the World Religions," in *From Max Weber: Essays in Sociology*, ed. H. H. Gerth and C. Wright Mills (New York: Oxford University Press, 1946), 275.

31. Max Weber, "Sociology of Religion," trans. Ephraim Fischoff, in *Economy and Society: An Outline of Interpretive Sociology*, ed. Guenther Roth and Claus Wittich (Berkeley: University of California Press, 1978), 523.

32. Martin Luther, *On the Bondage of the Will*, trans. and ed. Philip S. Watson with B. Drewery, *Luther and Erasmus: Free Will and Salvation* (Library of Christian Classics, Vol. XVII) (Philadelphia: Westminster, 1969), 330.

CHAPTER 3
Job Enacted

1. See Avigdor Shinan, "The Bible in the Synagogue"; Stefan C. Reif, "The Bible in the Liturgy"; "Table of Biblical Readings"; in *The Jewish Study Bible*, ed. Adele Berlin and Marc Zwi Brettler (New York and Oxford: Oxford University Press, 2004), 1929–37, 1937–48, 2115–17.

2. Ernst Dassmann, "Hiob," in *Reallexikon für Antike und Christentum*, ed. Ernst Dassmann, vol. 15 (Stuttgart: Anton Hiersemann, 1991), 366–442, 435–36

3. Dassmann, "Hiob," 438.

4. Louis Réau, *Iconographie de l'Art Chrétien* (Paris: PUF, 1956), 312.

5. Samuel Terrien, *The Iconography of Job through the Centuries: Artists as Biblical Interpreters* (University Park: Pennsylvania State University Press, 1996), 105ff.

6. G. Nepi Scirè and A. Gallo, *Chiesa di San Giobbe. Arte e devozione* (Venezia: Marsilio, 1994).

7. Dassman, "Hiob," 437; Barbara Nelson Sargent-
   Baur, *Brothers of Dragons: "Job Dolens" and
   François Villon* (New York: Garland Press, 1990),
   36. The book of Job did not play a comparable part
   in Eastern Christian traditions, perhaps because of
   Theodore of Mopsuestia's misgivings about all but
   the frame story. Selections from the frame story
   and theophany are read during Holy Week, and
   at least one tradition traces the words "Blessed be
   the name of the Lord" which end the Orthodox
   Divine Liturgy to Job. See St. Athanasius Academy
   of Orthodox Theology, *The Orthodox Study Bible*
   (Nashville: Thomas Nelson, 2008), 780–81, 814,
   819–20.

8. *Breviarum Romanum* (1829), 161; translation
   from the Douay-Rheims translation of the Vulgate.

9. Philippe Rouillard, "The Figure of Job in the
   Liturgy: Indignation, Resignation or Silence?" in
   Job and the Silence of God, ed. Christian Duquoc
   and Casiano Floristán (*Concilium*, Nov. 1983)
   (Edinburgh: T. & T. Clark; New York: Seabury,
   1983), 8–12, 11.

10. This lectionary is used by most Catholic and
    Protestant denominations in North America. See
    http://lectionary.library.vanderbilt.edu.

11. In the RCL Job 19:23–27a is also read once every
    three years during the season after Pentecost.

12. This is why these words are sung at the start of Part
    III of Handel's *Messiah*, the first heard after the
    "Hallelujah" chorus.

13. Translations are from the Douay-Rheims transla-
    tion of the Vulgate.

14. Rouillard, "The Figure of Job in the Liturgy," 9.

15. Catherine Pickstock, *After Writing: On the Liturgical Consummation of Philosophy* (Oxford and Malden, MA: Blackwell, 1998).

16. Rouillard, "The Figure of Job in the Liturgy," 11.

17. Stanzas 50, 53, lines 591–98, 626–31. See "Pety Job," in *Moral Love Songs and Laments*, ed. Susanna Greer Fein (Kalamazoo, MI: Medieval Institute Publications, 1998), http://www.lib .rochester.edu/camelot/petyfrm.htm.

18. Fein, "*Pety Job*: Introduction"; http://www.lib .rochester.edu/camelot/petyint.htm.

19. *La Pacience de Job. Mystère anonyme du XVe siècle*, ed. Albert Meiller (Paris: Klincksieck, 1971).

20. Besserman, *The Legend of Job in the Middle Ages*, 107.

21. *Pacience de Job*, lines 2268–87, cf. Besserman, *Legend of Job in the Middle Ages*, 98.

22. *Pacience de Job*, lines 3285–3329.

23. *Pacience de Job*, lines 5855–58.

24. *Pacience de Job*, lines 6230–31.

25. *Pacience de Job*, lines 6430–31.

26. *Pacience de Job*, line 6997.

27. Lucien Febvre, *The Problem of Unbelief in the Sixteenth Century: The Religion of Rabelais*, trans. Beatrice Gottlieb (Cambridge, MA: Harvard University Press, 1982), 336.

28. Simone Weil, *Waiting for God*, trans. Emma Craufurd (New York: Harper & Row, 1951), 135, 124. Weil's account of Job is given at 120–21.

29. Henri Lamarque, *L'Histoire de Griselda: une femme exemplaire dans les littératures européennes, tome 1: prose et poésie*, ed. Françoise Cazal, Raymond

Esclapez, Christophe Gonzalez, Henri Lamarque, Jean-Luc Nardone, and Yves Peyré (Toulouse: Presses Universitaires du Mirail, 2000), 11.

30. Ann W. Astell, "Translating Job as Female," in *Translation Theory and Practice in the Middle Ages*, ed. Jeanette Beer (Studies in Medieval Culture, 38) (Kalamazoo, MI: Medieval Institute Publications, 1997), 59–70.

31. Petrarch, "A Fable of Wifely Obedience and Devotion," trans. in Robert Dudley French ed., *A Chaucer Handbook*, 2nd ed. (New York: Appleton-Century-Crofts, 1947), 291–311, 310–11.

32. Petrarch, "A Fable of Wifely Obedience and Devotion," 311.

33. References are to line numbers in *The Riverside Chaucer*, 3rd. ed., ed. Larry D. Benson (Boston: Houghton Mifflin, 1987).

34. Edward I. Condren, "The Clerk's Tale of Man Tempting God," *Criticism* 26/2 (Spring 1984), 99–114: 100.

CHAPTER 4
Job in Theodicy

1. Hume, *Dialogues Concerning Natural Religion*, 63. Hume's source was Pierre Bayle, who found the otherwise unattested Epicurean trilemma in Lactantius' *De ira dei*. See my *The Problem of Evil: A Reader* (Oxford and Malden, MA: Blackwell, 2001), xviii–xxii, 46–52.

2. Arthur Lovejoy, *The Great Chain of Being: A Study of the History of an Idea* (Cambridge, MA: Harvard University Press, 1961), 208–10.

3. *Candide*, chapter 30; see *Candide*, trans., ed., and intro by Daniel Gordon (Boston and New York: Bedford/St. Martin's, 1999), 117.

4. *Candide*, chapter 30; trans. Gordon, 118.

5. Nancy Senior, "Voltaire and the Book of Job," *The French Review* 47/3 (December 1973): 340–47, 344.

6. Immanuel Kant, *Religion and Rational Theology*, ed. Allen W. Wood and trans. George di Giovanni (Cambridge and New York: Cambridge University Press, 2001), 26.

7. Hermann Cohen, *The Religion of Reason Out of the Sources of Judaism*, trans. Simon Kaplan (New York: Frederick Ungar, 1972), 226.

8. Emmanuel Levinas, "Useless Suffering," trans. Richard Cohen, in *The Provocation of Levinas: Rethinking the Other*, ed. Robert Bernasconi and David Wood (London and New York: Routledge, 1988), 156–67, 163.

9. Susan Neiman, *Evil in Modern Thought: An Alternative History of Philosophy* (Princeton: Princeton University Press, 2004).

10. J. G. Herder, *The Spirit of Hebrew Poetry*, trans. James Marsh, 2 vols. (Burlington: Edward Smith, 1833), I.120.

11. Jonathan Sheehan, *The Enlightenment Bible: Translation, Scholarship, Culture* (Princeton: Princeton University Press, 2005).

12. Robert Lowth, *Lectures on the Sacred Poetry of the Hebrews*, trans. G. Gregory, 2 vols. (London: J. Johnson, 1787; repr. London: Routledge/Thoemmes Press, 1995).

13. 39:9 is no longer translated as "unicorn" but as "wild ox." Behemoth (40:15–24) and Leviathan (41:1–34) may be based on the crocodile and hippopotamus.

14. Rudolf Otto, *The Idea of the Holy: An Inquiry into the Non-rational Factor in the Idea of the Divine and Its Relation to the Rational*, trans. John W. Harvey (New York: Oxford University Press, 1950), 78.

15. Lynn Poland, "*The Idea of the Holy* and the history of the sublime," *Journal of Religion* 72/2 (April 1992): 175–97.

16. G. K. Chesterton, Introduction to *The Book of Job* (London: Cecil Palmer & Hayward, 1916), ix–xxvii, xvi.

17. Slavoj Žižek and John Milbank, *The Monstrosity of Christ: Paradox or Dialectic?* ed. Creston Davis (Cambridge, MA and London: MIT Press, 2009), 54–56.

18. See Bo Lindberg, *William Blake's Illustrations to the Book of Job* (Turku, Finland: Abo Akademi, 1973).

19. Christopher Rowland, *Blake and the Bible* (New Haven, CT: Yale University Press, 2010), 5.

20. David Brown, *Discipleship and Imagination: Christian Tradition and Truth* (Oxford: Oxford University Press, 2000), 221.

21. 2 Cor 3:6 and 1 Cor 2:14. S. Foster Damon, *Blake's "Job": Blake's "Illustrations of the Book of Job"* (Providence, RI: Brown University Press, 1966), 55.

22. 1 John 3:2; John 14:9; John 10:30; John 14:20. (Damon, *Blake's "Job,"* 63–64).

23. "Blake's reading of the Book of Job," in *Northrop Frye on Milton and Blake*, ed. Angela Esterhammer (Toronto, Buffalo, London: University of Toronto Press, 2005), 387–401, 392.

CHAPTER 5
Job in Exile

1. Harold Kushner, *The Book of Job: When Bad Things Happened to a Good Person* (New York: Schocken, 2012), 15.

2. See Zuckerman, *Job the Silent: A Study in Historical Counterpoint*.

3. Newsom, *The Book of Job: A Contest of Moral Imaginations*.

4. Marvin Pope, *The Anchor Bible: Job* (Garden City, NY: Doubleday & Co., 1965), xviii.

5. Robert Alter, *The Wisdom Books* (New York and London: Norton, 2010), 106–110, 6.

6. Samuel ben Nissim Masnuth argued to this effect already in the twelfth century CE; *Jewish Study Bible*, 1501.

7. James Kugel, *The Great Poems of the Bible: A Reader's Companion with New Translations* (New York: Free Press, 2008), 105.

8. F. Delitzsch, *Biblical Commentary on the Book of Job*, trans. Francis Bolton, 2 vols. (Edinburgh: T & T Clark, 1866, 1869), 2:114.

9. Nahum H. Glatzer, *Baeck-Buber-Rosenzweig Reading the Book of Job: Leo Baeck Memorial Lecture 10* (New York: Leo Baeck Institute, 1966).

10. Habtu, "Introduction to the Wisdom Literature," *Africa Bible Commentary*, 569.

11. Raymond Scheindlin, *The Book of Job* (New York: W. W. Norton, 1999). Another recent poetic translator, Robert Alter, assesses the poetic value of Elihu differently, thinking it inferior to the rest of the book.

12. Newsom, *Book of Job*, chap. 8.

13. Cynthia Ozick, "The Impious Impatience of Job," in *The Best American Essays 1999*, ed. Edward Hoagland, 201–11 (Boston and New York: Houghton Mifflin, 1999), 209.

14. Kugel, *How to Read the Bible*, 673–74.

15. This argument is made by Peter L. Berger in *The Heretical Imperative: Contemporary Possibilities of Religious Affirmation* (Garden City, NY: Anchor Press, 1979) and underlies Charles Taylor's *A Secular Age* (Cambridge, MA: Harvard University Press, 2007).

16. Nahum N. Glatzer, *The Dimensions of Job: A Study and Selected Readings* (New York: Schocken, 1969) and, more generally, Besterman, *Legend of Job*.

17. René Girard, *Job: The Victim of His People* (Stanford: Stanford University Press, 1987).

18. David Rosenberg, *A Literary Bible: An Original Translation* (Berkeley: Counterpoint, 2009), 432. Cf. Job 16:18–19.

19. Fyodor Dostoyevsky, *The Brothers Karamazov*, trans. David Magarshack (Harmondsworth: Penguin, 1982), 343.

20. See Clines, "Why Is There a Book of Job and What Does It Do to You If You Read It?"

21. http://www.nobelprize.org/nobel_prizes/peace /laureates/1986/wiesel-lecture.html.

NOTES TO CHAPTER 5

22. Elie Wiesel, *Night*, 42; quoted in Néher, *The Exile of the Word*, 220.

23. Elie Wiesel, *Legends of Our Time* (New York, Chicago, San Francisco: Holt, Rinehart and Winston, 1968), 97.

24. Elie Wiesel, *The Town Beyond the Wall*, 52; quoted in Néher, *The Exile of the Word*, 223.

25. Elie Wiesel, "Job," in *Peace, In Deed: Essays in Honor of Harry James Cargas*, ed. Zev Garber and Richard Libowitz (Atlanta: Scholars Press, 1998), 119–34, 124.

26. Wiesel, *Legends of Our Time*, viii.

27. Elie Wiesel, *Célébration Biblique* (1975), translated by Marion Wiesel as *Messengers of God: Biblical Portraits and Legends* (New York: Random House, 1996).

28. Elie Wiesel, *Messengers of God*, 213.

29. http://www.nobelprize.org/nobel_prizes/peace/laureates/1986/wiesel-lecture.html.

30. Wiesel, "Job," in *Peace, In Deed*, 134.

31. Wiesel, "Job," in *Peace, In Deed*, 133.

32. Wiesel, "Job," in *Peace, In Deed*, 130.

33. Beal, *The Rise and Fall of the Bible*, 167.

34. Wiesel, "Job," in *Peace, In Deed*, 134.

35. Richard Rubenstein, "Job and Auschwitz," in *Strange Fire: Reading the Bible after the Holocaust*, ed. Tod Lingafelt (New York: NYU Press, 2000), 233–51: 242.

36. Rubenstein, "Job and Auschwitz."

37. See Néher, *Exile of the Word*.

38. Margarete Susman, *Das Buch Hiob und das Schicksal des jüdischen Volkes* (Freiburg: Herder, 1968), 217.

39. In the second, 1948, edition of her book Susman acknowledged the miracle of the establishment of the state of Israel but lamented the new nation's military might. The young pioneers should be honored and supported, but the rest of the Jewish people must continue to represent the rejection of war and the temptations of territorial nationalism.

40. "Das Hiob-Problem bei Franz Kafka," *Der Morgen* 1 (April 1929): 31–49; http://www.margaretesusman .com/hiobproblemkafka.htm.

41. Schreiner, *Where Shall Wisdom Be Found?* 189.

42. Taylor, *A Secular Age*.

Conclusion

1. Newsom, *Book of Job*, 29.

2. Nelly Sachs, "Hiob," in *Spiegelungen: Biblische Texte und modern Lyrik*, ed. Johann Hinrich Claussen (Zürich: Pano, 2004), 57.

3. Ethan and Joel Coen, directors, *A Serious Man*, 2009. Terrence Malick, director, *The Tree of Life*, 2011.

4. André Kabasele Mukenge, "Une lecture populaire de la figure de Job au Congo," *Bulletin for Old Testament Studies in Africa*, May 16, 2004: 2–6.

5. Tewoldemedhin Habtu, "Job," *Africa Bible Commentary*, 572.

6. Gerald O. West and Bongi Zengele, "Reading Job 'Positively' in the Context of HIV/AIDS in South

Africa," *Job's God*, ed. E. J. van Wolde (London: SCM Press, 2004), 112–24.

7. Sarojini Nadar, "'*Barak* God and Die!' Women, HIV and a Theology of Suffering," in *Grant Me Justice! HIV/AIDS and Gender Readings of the Bible*, ed. Musa W. Dube and Musimbi R. A. Kanyoro (Maryknoll, NY: Orbis, 2004), 60–79.

8. Zakia Pathak, "A Pedagogy for Postcolonial Feminists," in *The Postmodern Bible Reader*, ed. David Jobling, Tina Pippin, and Ronald Schleifer (Oxford and Malden, MA: Blackwell, 2001), 217–32, 222.

9. Gustavo Gutiérrez, *On Job: God-Talk and the Suffering of the Innocent*, trans. Matthew O'Connell (Maryknoll, NY: Orbis, 1987).

10. D.J.A. Clines, "Why is there a Book of Job . . . ?"

11. Elsa Tamez, "Dear Brother Job . . . A letter from the dump," *Sojourners* 12/8 (September 1983): 23.

INDEX LOCORUM

language: archaized in prose
    frame narrative, 11, 198–99;
    contradiction as revelatory
    of truth, 69–70; failure of,
    181, 222; figurative, *31*; *hapax
    legomena* and obscurity of
    text, 6; homonyms, 52–53, 57,
    60–61; inadequacy of, 248; as
    magical gift in *The Testament
    of Job*, 46; philology and
    historical criticism, 196–97.
    See also speech; translation
Leaman, Oliver, 184
Legends of the Jews (Ginzberg), 49
Leibniz, Gottfried Wilhelm,
    158–59
Leningrad Codex, *52–53*
Leviathan, 3, *31*, 70, 135, 161, 207,
    261n13
Lewis, C. S., 71
liberation theology, 245–46
literacy, 32–33
literal readings, 39, 82; Aquinas
    and, 95–96; biblical literal-
    ism, 18, 208–10; Blake and,
    192; Calvin and, 115; rejected
    by Gregory I, 65–66, 69
liturgies, book of Job and,
    117–22; breviaries and,
    119–20; Office of the Dead
    and, 21, 121–22, 125–34,
    140; in Revised Common
    Lectionary, 120
lost text passages, 9, 202
Lowth, Robert, 11, 174–77
Luther, Martin, 37–38, 114, 157,
    256n21

MacLeish, Archibald, 87
Maimonides, 83–95, 114–15;
    Baba Bathra referenced by,

85, 86, 93; and Job as parable,
    57; negation in, 84, 90–94;
    and parabolic reading, 57,
    84–87, 91–94, 115
"The Marriage of Heaven and
    Hell" (Blake), 192–93
Masoretes, 6, 7, 52
material reality: Gregory and re-
    jection of materiality, 74–75;
    historical carnal/allegorical
    spiritual in Gregory, 73–75
melancholy, 156–57
Metamorphosis (Kafka), 236–37
midrashim: questioning and,
    49–51, 64, 227–28; *The Testa-
    ment of Job* as midrash, 49;
    Wiesel and textual inquiry as
    midrash, 225–28
Milton, John, 159–60, 188
Milton (Blake), 186–88
missing text, 9, 202
Mitchell, Stephen, 19, 184, 205
Moralia / Morals in Job
    (Gregory the Great), 29, 32,
    65–76
Mu'tazila, 90
mysteriousness, 178–79

nature, 3, 174, 178; Blake's
    use of nature or animal
    imagery, 189; as evidence of
    divine creation, 79–80; free
    will of creation, 90; God's
    relationship to forces of, 86;
    as instrument of God, 61–62;
    material world as analog to
    spiritual, 245; suffering as
    natural event, 93–94. *See also*
    animals
negation, 84, 90–94
Néher, André, 230